# My Gift to You

This book is presented as a Gift to:

_____

From:

_____

Date:

_____

"Happily Ever After" is Within Your Reach

*"Happily Ever After" is Within Your Reach.*
*The Journey Begins with You.*
Learn How Not to Make the Biggest Mistakes of Your Life.


*J. B. Love*

# How to Find, Enjoy & Keep Real Love

*(A Common Sense Guide to a Healthy Relationship)*

By
*J. B. Love*

# Disclaimer

This book is a "common sense" guide to a healthy relationship. The author wrote about her experiences in her life, the advice she received, and actions she observed. The discussions in this book are things she has seen work or fail consistently over the years. It is worth the read. Some might read this book and find it very judgmental in regards their lifestyle. However, the author is an advocate for children; therefore, any suggestions that were given that involves a child or will/could affect them in the future is always her point of view in the best interest of a child and not anyone else. The author understands that we all fall but what defines us is how we rise after falling. She is pluralistic and respects the difference in races and religions. She feels that we all belong to the human race, and her humanity is as such. Although she speaks about the doctrine of her faith, she understands that there is sound doctrine found in other religions as well.

This book is not as a substitute for the advice of a marriage, relationship or abuse counselor. The sale of this book by the author and publisher is not rendering psychological, financial, legal, or other professional services. If expert assistance or counseling is needed, the reader should consult a licensed professional. Any application of the material in the following pages is at the reader's discretion and sole responsibility.

The author and publisher have made every effort to ensure that the information in this book was correct at press time. The author and publisher do not assume and hereby disclaim any liability to any party for any loss, damage, or disruption caused by errors or omissions, whether such errors or omissions result from negligence, accident, or any other cause. This book has scenarios and recreate events and conversations from the author's memories of them. To maintain anonymity, she has omitted all names of individuals and places.

# Contents

# *Acknowledgement*

*To all that have provided inspiration and /or made this project possible: I Acknowledge You!*

Cover Photo Designed by Freepik

**HOW TO FIND, ENJOY, & KEEP REAL LOVE**

# Dedication

I dedicate this book to my readers. I hope to inspire and have a lasting relationship with them. Also, I dedicate this book to myself for learning to love myself and finally realizing that I have a platinum heart that is beautiful that desires to spend time with people who uplift me and enhances the amazing person that I am so that I can shine and empower others to make the world a better place.

*Without loving myself and wanting the best for you,*
*this could not have been possible.*

Above all, I am grateful to God who has given me the ability to express myself through words. He also blessed with wonderful parents, Carl and Earie, and I am indebted to my many family members and friends who encouraged me along the way. I cannot thank them all enough. To all of the above I dedicate the following verse:

## My Colorful World

*A world without you would be a world without color.*
*May you continue to inspire me to paint my world a masterpiece.*

***HOW TO FIND, ENJOY, & KEEP REAL LOVE***

# Introduction

I am back with another project, *How to Find, Enjoy and Keep Real Love (A Common Sense Guide to a Healthy Relationship)*. I hope you enjoyed *Anticipation—10 Keys to Turning Your Dreams into Reality and Love, Life and Courage (Poetry for the Soul)*. I wrote this book based on the poems contained in the Love section of *Love, Life and Courage (Poetry for the Soul)*. It is my experiences, observation, and the results of interviews regarding relationships.

This is more than just your average book. Learn how not to make the worst mistakes of your life. Through the use of a common sense guide to a healthy relationship, you will be taken on a journey of discovery that will lead you to find yourself and to take the necessary steps toward finding and enjoying that someone special and living your life to its fullest on your terms. I say on your terms because many times others feel you are not living life to its fullest if it is not on their terms.

This book looks at love and the challenges we all go through in life in relationships. I wrote it to inspire you to become a better you through the choices you make in life. The choices we make in life leads us to our destiny. My son often asked my husband and me when he was younger, "Daddy and Momma how did you find each other?" Because I love to hear my husband's version of our story, I always would let him answer. My husband always tells him that he found me after traveling the world and looking in all the wrong places. He has always said to me over the years that he still enjoys being with me and having me in his life. Do you want to know what real love is and how to find, enjoy and keep it? Read on and I will share my knowledge on where to get started and how to create a healthy relationship that will have a greater chance of surviving the bitter storms of life.

Life is not a dream and rarely mimics Utopia.

There is no perfect place or society
where we can find perfect people
except on the big screen, in our imagination
and in our dreams.

# Chapter One

## Live Your Dream of Happily Ever After

Most people have dreamed of living a fairytale at one time or another. We all have dreamed of meeting our prince charming, our king or our queen; however, life is not a fairytale and rarely mimics Utopia. There is no perfect place or society where we can find perfect people except on the big screen, our imagination and in our dreams; however, some dreams can and do come true with preparation and work. I am not talking about any work. We all have seen people working hard at the wrong things in life. The type of work that is needed to make a relationship successful has to be the right actions. With the right actions, you can live your dreams and turn them into realities.

The problem with finding, enjoying, and keeping real love is that some spend more time and energy on the wrong things in life and their risk factors for failure are many. A successful relationship involves a commitment from both parties to their self and each other. Marriage is more than the rehearsal dinner, the ceremony on the big wedding day, and the honeymoon. It is legally binding. It is a contractual relationship between two people recognized by law and a vow made before God. Therefore, it should not be entered into lightly or hastily without a review of yourself, the other person, the situation, and how you will go about blending two into one and maintaining. It is an investment worth protecting. In living your dreams, you should seek to prevent as many nightmare factors as possible on the front end. It will make your journey through life easier.

# A Common Sense Recipe for Real Everlasting Love

Oh, the quest for real everlasting love! "Forever Together" what a concept. To love and be loved is what every heart desires. Some people live their whole life feeling they have never experienced either; however, this experience can be achieved, and it is truly rewarding. Although my husband and I have had some bad as well as good times because of the choices we made, key things have kept our relationship healthy and strong over the years plus there are a few things that would have made our journey easier had we followed them. These essential, fundamental principles involved building a solid foundation and structure and maintaining our relationship. I refer to it as our "House of Love." I call these fundamental principles "A Common Sense Recipe for Real Everlasting Love":

## A Common Sense Recipe for Real Everlasting Love

*Essential Ingredients Needed for Finding, Enjoying & Keeping Real Love:*

### Building a Solid Foundation & Structure
Avoid Factors that Increase the Risk of Relationship Failure
Love and Be Your Best Self
Be Approachable
Get to Know the Other Person
Recognize Dysfunction and Choose the Right Situation
Choose the Right Mate for You

### Maintaining Your "House of Love"
Have the Acronym TRUST
Put in the Work
Pay Attention to the Signs

Combine all the above ingredients. Add enough spice to fuel the fire as hot as the two of you can stand. Like with any recipe, every long lasting relationship is different and you will need to add that special ingredient that makes it your own. I define "spice" as whatever attraction(s) were used in the beginning and whatever spices you two decide to explore together. It needs to be your special ingredient that you add to the mix. You should continue these throughout the relationship. Cover and simmer indefinitely.

**The ingredients will yield a healthy proportion of quality, longevity and real love in your "House of Love".**

These common sense ingredients have been things I have seen work or fail if they were missing over the years in relationships consistently. These ideas are not complicated. Most of them except for the grownup ones are things we should have learned as children in elementary, playing on the playground or in Sunday School. Remember the Golden Rule *(common sense ethics)*, Dr. Seuss' children book series, and The Ten Commandments *(if you are Christian)* just to name a few. These concepts were all about how to treat others, to treat and believe in yourself, to conduct yourself, and to stay safe *(i.e. avoid risks that do not contribute to a good life)*. It is incredible how our lives would be better if we as adults follow some of the things we learned as children.

*You must first build a solid foundation and structure for love that will withstand the bitter storms of life.*

# Chapter Two

# Find Real Love by Building a Solid Foundation & Structure

Contrary to popular belief, happy and healthy relationships and marriages can and do exist. Just like building a house, you must also build a healthy relationship that will last. Do you remember the London fairy tale from the 1890s, "The Three Little Pigs" that your parents read to you as a child, or you read in grade school? It consisted of three little pigs that went into the world and they each built a house for shelter for protection from the "big bad wolf". In this book, the big bad wolf will represent life's challenges that you will encounter in your quest for "happily ever after". These three pigs that were siblings I will refer to as Lazy, Mediocre, and Visionary. They built houses out of straw, stick, and brick, respectively. Lazy, who was in denial, built a house out of straw because he was disinclined to work hard but wanted to reap all the benefits. Mediocre knew that Lazy's plan was flawed and would have problems, but he did not want to go too far against the current grain and take the necessary actions to break the cycle; therefore, he built a house that was only moderate and lacking exceptional quality. Visionary was a hard worker and was sometimes picked on for his values and ethics; however, he had the good common sense to know that he needed to find the best materials for the time, bricks, if his house was going to have exceptional quality and last. What kind of real estate on your quest of finding lasting love will you make your investment? We have all heard of "Location, Location, Location" as it relates to real estate. Have you been putting yourself in the best locations (*i.e. environments*) regarding your real estate of life?

In your "House of Love", you must first build a solid foundation and structure for love that will withstand the bitter storms of life. You need the first six essential ingredients to build that foundation and structure. Now, let us take a look at these essential ingredients in more detail in the next sections.

---

*If the risk does not contribute to a good life,*

*it is not worth taking.*

## 2:1 Avoid Factors that Increase the Risk of Relationship Failure

Now it's time to discuss how not to make some of the biggest mistakes of your life. Before you can get started with living your dream of "Happily Ever After", you must first avoid the pitfalls which are risks that are more likely than not to wreck your dreams. These pitfalls are common sense known factors that increase the likelihood of relationship failure. Some will be discussed in detail in the other chapters and sections of this book:

- **No religious affiliation** – Regardless of the religion, each doctrine has guidelines that are good blueprints designed to reduce risks in all aspects of life. These guidelines add to the moral fabric of society. I am of the Christian faith, and we have The Ten Commandments along with other sound principles found in the BIBLE, which can be seen as B.I.B.L.E. *(Basic Instructions Before Leaving Earth)*. It has been either my personal experience or my observation that when Christians' life reflects these guidelines and principles, their risks of social ills and their consequences are avoided or reduced. Our actions have consequences in life either good or bad. The bad brings drama and chaos to our lives that we do not need that hinder our goals which aids in the decay of society. Although you cannot entirely avoid sin in life, it is an excellent practice to keep our thoughts and actions to a standard contained in the guidelines of doctrines. Our thoughts will our words and actions. They are good goals for which to strive and you will find that it will make your journey through life easier and more rewarding.

- **Becoming pregnant before marriage** – Beyond religion, there are valid common sense reasons why becoming pregnant before marriage is a bad idea. First, marriage itself can be challenging; especially if you have not chosen right. Now, add a child to the mix to start off. After becoming pregnant and having a child, the child becomes the priority. Any dreams or plans you had for yourself before will need to take a back seat. Ideally, if the participants of a marriage choose right, marriage is the best place for pregnancies. I will tell you later in this book what I mean by choosing right. Second, let's talk about sex. You become pregnant before marriage by having sex. Sex has consequences. They are good or bad depending on your situation. The number one consequence is unwanted pregnancies. Although used for pleasure, sex was designed for procreation. Sometimes, those pleasure attempts turn into procreation. In most cases, UNWANTED pregnancies by at least one participant. We all know a few OOPs babies. Most times it does not lead to marriage. The majority of them do not get to share a home in which both of their parents live, and their parents never get married. Some never even see their fathers or even know their fathers. `Abstinence, the practice of restraining oneself from indulging in something *(i.e. sex)*, is the only 100% method of not becoming pregnant. Condoms, when used improperly or properly, have a failure rate that not only leads to pregnancies but diseases as well. Other birth control methods have failure rates and present potential health issues for the users.

Beyond unwanted pregnancies, sex outside of marriage has other RISKs. I have two words, Disease, and Death. Diseases which can not only cause sterility if not caught in time but the disease which causes death *(AIDS)* and there is the death of dreams. Currently, I know of four people who had died of AIDS and a couple of individuals who cannot have children. There is no need to discuss these any further as they are self-explanatory. You only get one life. It is in your and your further family's best interest to maximize its potential.

Becoming pregnant before marriage does not constitute love is not a surefire way to the altar. It's time for Sex Education 101. Now it is time to share what I learned from my mother, grandmother, in my grade school home-economics and college health classes. Love does not create or produce a baby. In the traditional sense, heterosexual intercourse involving penetration of the vagina of a female by the penis of a male and the ejaculation of sperm by a male that fertilizes an egg of a female produces a baby. While it may seem silly for me to have to state the above facts, some people by their actions have forgotten Sex Education 101 and often confuse "lust" with "love". Lust is the overwhelming attraction and actions to fulfill one's sexual desires with no regard for the consequences. In lust, people's heart seeks one thing in mind, sex. Sex has consequences that present problems for the participants; especially if they are not married. In love, there are two peoples' minds with each other's best interest at heart. You fall in love so two hearts can rise in that love together as one. Lust does not require any deep affection as love does. Lust begets loneliness while love begets love. People, when someone whispers "I Love You," where does it say in that sentence "only"; especially if there are no actions that reflect love. Gold diggers and gigolos know this, and they do not love you. They just want something from you. If your resources are plenty, most gold diggers either want to be "kept" or are just looking for a payday every month for the next 18 years or 24 years if the child goes to college and most gigolos just want to be kept and travel the world and "hit it" in every city. At least, that is what the female gold diggers and male gigolos I asked told me about their situations. Often these days when people become pregnant before marriage and get married because of it, it is not real love and usually does not last. This book is talking about how to find, enjoy and keep real love. It is talking about how to make your journey through life easier not harder. Ladies, if you only see him from midnight to 6 a.m. (usually jump off hours); especially if he never brings you home and your work schedule does not conflict, it's not love and why would you want a baby by a man who does not love you and you are not married too. A lot of times the man is actually in love with someone else. Just because someone desires to have sex with you, that does not mean that they love you. More likely than not, they want and love sex.

When people marry in these type of situations, they either got married because:

1.  their partner in lust did not wish to pay child support outside a home he was not going to be living in

2.  they wanted to save their self and family embarrassment; especially if they were supposed to be practicing some religious belief

3.  they were pressured or forced to getting married

4.  maybe they grew up without a father in the home and did not want the unborn child to experience the same thing

The reason for the marriage does not matter. It is not love, and the marriage will reflect it. A baby or child does not keep a man. In some women's case, it does not get a man. We already know the situation is not ideal and if the two of them are not compatible there will not be much enjoyment in the relationship. If there is no love, this produces a problem for all involved at this point and in the future including the child. Like my mother and grandmother used to say, it takes a village to raise a child and if possible, a child deserves to grow up in a home with two loving parents. It is crucial for their growth and development. Children just deserve more. We can sit and make excuses all day long that would make this type of activity appropriate; however, I grew up with children from these type of situations, and they told me about their pain and how fortunate I was in my life. I could see the hurt in them, and it was a lot different than what their parents were preaching. You see, sometimes a parent's reality and their children reality are two separate things. I recently heard a television talk show where some of the hosts appeared to be criticizing a young woman who had a hashtag on her birthday cake that read "#35 and No Baby Daddy". The question up for debate was whether there was something wrong with having a "baby daddy" and being single (as if the woman's birthday cake offended the "baby mommas" of the world).

One of the hosts said that she thought it was O.K. to decide to have a baby outside of marriage if that's what you want to do; however, this decision should not be based on what you as an individual want to do. It should be about what would be in the best interest of the child.

- **Living together before marriage** – When you play grown people games, grown things happen, like pregnancies before the marriage. These pregnancies usually occur between people who never make it to the altar. There is less sense of commitment in some people that are just living together also known as "shacking" as opposed to them being married. In a sense, they can have their cake and eat it too. How many times have you heard a person, say "he or she *(referring to someone they are living with)* don't have any papers on me?" I know of a man who lived with at least three different women one of which he had several kids by to add to the list of kids he already had created with other women that he was not taking care of properly. He never married either of the women he lived with but married one of the women he was seeing while he was living with one of the others. She did not live with him prior before they decided to get married nor did she have a baby by him. Common sense should tell everyone that their significant other needs to put a ring on it *(as in actually getting married)* or they need to keep it moving. Do not fall for "you would not buy a car without test driving it first" foolishness. How many car dealers do you know that would allow you to test drive a car for years before you purchased it? Selling the car to someone else would be difficult. They certainly couldn't sell it new especially considering the miles on it.

- **No preparation before marriage** – Before couples get married they should have marriage counseling. Some couples spend more time planning for a wedding rather than planning for their future. Instead of preparing for a wedding right off the bat, they should plan their life together. A marriage counselor can easily facilitate this. When you are dating someone; especially if it's been only for a very short time, you are not seeing the real person. A lot of time they are just giving you what they "think" you want to get you. It is not who they are as a person. The real person is usually revealed sometime later and most times for a lot of people it is after dating.

There are some basic questions that you will learn later in this book that the both of you need to know the answers to before you jump the broom. These issues usually are addressed in counseling sessions. Sometimes couples find out in counseling that they simply are just not compatible and are not the right person for each other. Since you cannot be sure how the sessions will go, it is also advisable that you attend counseling before you announce your engagement. You should view marriage counseling as a positive thing. The best thing that could happen to you is that you find out you prevented the worst mistake of your life by marrying the wrong person for you.

A marriage is not some magical potion that creates real love. That only exists in fairytales. Therefore, when people rush into it or trick someone into it who they do not know, are not compatible with, and are not already in love with, it usually does not last long. If it does, it is not healthy as those years are often filled with heartache, pain, and suffering.

- **Marrying at a very early age** – When people marry at a very young age, they have not had all the experiences in life they should have before settling down and are not mature enough to handle the challenges *(bitter storms in life)* of life that occur during a marriage. They have not had sufficient time to prepare their selves for these challenges. They have not gotten all the things out of their system they need to before marriage and children. In this day and age, no one should marry anyone before the age of 25. At least, by age 25 if you are on the right track you should have completed your education *(formal or informal and non-traditional or traditional from an accredited college)*, partied until you have just about dropped if you are of the partying kind, traveled, and been in the workforce for several years. I am speaking from experience and observation here, and I chose the age 25 for specific reasons beyond the experiences you must have before marriage: (1) Health reasons if you plan to have more than one child. If you want to start a family, your chances of success *(percentages)* regarding procreation is greater in your twenties than in your thirties and forties. The percentage drops as the woman and her eggs age. I know a few women who got married in my thirties and had a difficult time. That is not to say everyone will have a difficult time but there are studies out there you can go and read that speaks to this known fact. A woman's body can snap back into shape quicker when she is younger. Other health problems are more frequent in pregnant older women than young women & etc. (2) Except for exceptions, you have more energy to deal with a little one(s) and your mate when you are younger. (3) When your kids grow up and leave home, you will still have the energy to enjoy yourself. (4) When your children have their kids, you will still have the energy to be active grandparents. I heard a little boy say it best. One day he told me, "when I grow up, I don't want to wait until I am in my late thirties or forties to have kids. The majority of the time, daddy and pawpaw *(his grandfather)* are not able to keep up in sports and etc." In his case, he was correct. His mom was in her thirties, and her husband was five years older than her. Now add six to ten years to that about the age when sons can do things with fathers and grandfathers that put his father and grandfather in their fifties and seventies. I am not saying that when you reach the age 25, you should marry out of fear because the "clock is ticking". From a common sense standpoint approach, all I am saying is that choices in life have consequences, and you need to be aware of them and accept whatever the consequences are for the choices you make.

- **Your significant other coming from long line of dysfunctional family situations** in the family they grew up in; including their birth family not knowing how to stay out of their grown family members' personal business. The problem is that they see their behavior as normal and anyone else as evil and crazy. Dysfunction is a major risk factor for a healthy and happy relationship or marriage. People typically behave the way they have been taught to act by the examples they have had in their lives. You and your mate must be equally yoked. I will discuss this in detail in another section of this book. There is some validity to being equally yoked and avoiding dysfunctionality.

- **No or less income and education** – A marriage cannot survive on love alone. You cannot support a family if the financial resources are not there. Not having the resources will put a strain on your marriage like no other. I am not talking about the extra money needed for those much-needed vacations to just get away from the everyday hustle and bustle stresses of life. When you cannot meet the basic needs of survival like water, food, shelter, and medical care which requires income you can't possibly deal with any other challenges that may arise in a marriage. Your level of education *(academic or vocational)* will dictate your earning potential in life. Educated people who are self-sufficient tend to make better choices and decisions in life.

- **Feelings of insecurity** – Less just face it, people who are in relationships and marriages not based on real love but based on trickery are always insecure. Therefore, their actions which usually are not good reflect it. They are afraid of losing the person as the love was never really there. Also, people who are not confident and have very low self-esteem are always insecure. It's hard for a person with low self-esteem to love others when they do not love their self.

In your quest for "Happy Ever After", it is common sense that real love, preparation, and effort should fill a serious relationship or marriage for it to be healthy and everlasting. People often ask me, "What is the secret to the longevity of my husband and my marriage?" In addition to longevity, I like to talk about health or quality of a relationship. Later you will learn why longevity should not be the only measure of a successful or healthy relationship or marriage. The real secret is that there is no secret. It is good common sense, love, and hard work. You get out of something what you put into it. Therefore, if no preparation and common sense went into in on the front end, it is not likely to last. If it does last, it is not likely to be successful or healthy.

You will always be one-half of every relationship you will ever enter into with someone. Investing in yourself will be one of the best returns on investment you will ever make in your life.

You will attract people based on who they perceive you to be. Four great traits to have are to be:

1  Loving
2  Self-sufficient
3  Secure
4  Confident

## 2:2   Love and Be Your Best Self

Before you start your quest for finding your prince charming, your king or your queen, you must first find yourself. "Happily Ever After" begins with you. A healthy relationship always starts and ends with you. Every house needs a good foundation to withstand the test of times. In your "House of Love", loving and being your best self will be part of your stable foundation. You must always remember that you will always be one-half of every relationship that you will ever enter into with someone. Therefore, if you want a healthy relationship, you must bring a healthy "you" in mind, body, and spirit to the table. You cannot enter into a relationship expecting the other person to be a miracle worker and make you a healthy, happy, and a loving person if you are not. A healthy "you" will always be your calm during the storms.

Beware of people who tell you to think like someone else. You should forget about thinking like or acting like anyone else other than yourself. I was at a salon once, and a person was talking about this concept and was saying "finally" as if some light had turned on in her head. It was somewhat strange to me because I was aware of the man she was dating and what was on his mind. Thinking "like" him was not going to help her, and it did not as they were seeking two different things from their relationship. Sometimes people in relationships have different realities. You should be careful about taking relationship advice from someone who appears to have a one-sided view of what a good relationship is or who has never been in a good or healthy relationship for any length of time. You know some of us have friends who have been in one relationship after another and do not currently have anyone, or they have someone they do not know but will not hesitate to give you advice as if it is the gospel. Misery loves company. It should be like wanting to become a millionaire and seeking advice from a millionaire. If you wish to have a healthy relationship, you should seek advice from people who have been in good relationships. Sure a person who has been in one bad relationship after another can tell you plenty about not doing the wrong things but do they know enough about the "good, good" to balance it out. We will discuss the "good, good" later. Only abstaining from the bad will not be enough. You will need to know how to bring the "good and plenty."

You should never pretend to be someone you are not. If you keep pretending you will get caught up and remember it's you, you forgot. You must love yourself enough to be yourself. You will attract people based on who they perceive you to be. Like birds of a feather, people flock to those they think are what they are looking for in a mate. Therefore, if you are pretending eventually, the other person will find you out. When people are pretending to be someone they are not, at some point, they usually stop pretending. The majority of the time when people say people have changed in a relationship what has happened is that they are not pretending anymore, and they reveal their real character. The person's character they now see is the actual character from the very start. People do not have to pretend, they are special simply because they are and that is what makes them unique. There is truly someone for everyone, and you need the one for you and not the one for someone else. You will find the one for you by being yourself and not by creating illusions of someone else. To just "be it" and "do it" is far better than having the "illusion of it". One of the biggest things I hate is when women say they want a real man and real love; yet, they are not real themselves. When a man falls for the illusion of them then turns around and strays or leaves when the truth the real person is revealed, they get mad. A man spots a woman that he thinks is his type because she is trying to be and is doing all the things she either knows he like or thinks he like. After he gets her home, she removes the butt and breast pads, the colored contact lenses, and the weave *(or it comes out during sex when he tries to run his fingers through it or pulls on it)*. Now she and her real traits are revealed. He starts to stray or leave and the woman gets upset. Well, he is still looking for that woman he thought you were. I must say this about hair before moving on. I know that today *(except for the case of cancer survivors)* weaves and wigs are fashion accessories; however, there are some men that have a thing for either naturally long or short hair. It is a turn on to them. When I was younger, there was this guy who wanted to date me that had an obsession with women with short hair. There was such an obsession that he asked me if I would cut my hair. I just said, "no" and kept it moving. When someone pointed out his ex-girlfriend to me, one day, I finally understood why. Here was a woman that had left him and didn't want him anymore and he was trying to create the image of her in someone else.

On the other hand, a woman meets a man, and he presents himself as single, available, loving and successful. Later, she finds out he is married *(or separated as some like to say)* and has children by one or sometimes several women. He can't afford to take care of any of them including himself and lives with his momma or boys. He is loving or in this case "hitting" everything within his grasp. If she is smart, she starts to run, and he get mad and start stalking &, etc. Fellas, be honest up front there is someone out there for you too, and that is who you need to find. I know you think most women say they want to hear the truth, but when you tell the truth, they can't handle the truth. Well, the right one for you will be able to handle it. I know plenty of females who will help pull half-a-man out the gutter and take care of him and live with all his drama. You always hear these same ladies loudly bragging about how they "let a man be a man" *(their perception of what constitutes a real man)*. They then say while he is with his boys and doing "his thang," I'm doing "my thang" with my girls only to discover later his boys was another woman or women who some come up pregnant. You can note that sometimes she is not actually with her girls, and, at least, one or more of those kids you think are yours is someone else. I know from experience, if a real man feels or knows you are the one for him, you will not have to chase him or pull him out of someone else's bed as he will automatically want to be where ever you are. Beware of naysayers. People can say what they want to say; however, I speak the truth here. One of the finest men *(body and heart)* on this planet asked to "put a ring on it" before he test drove anything. He saw in me the woman he had been looking for all his adult life and wanted to spend the rest of his life with me. He explicitly told me that he prayed to God for someone just like me. He found me while I was living my best life and being my best self. I was the woman my God intended me to be. If it can happen to me, it can happen to you.

You should conduct an examination of yourself. Many times when people move from one relationship to the next continually, it is not the other person. You need to do three things: (1) Recall (2) Discover & Take Action and (3) Avoid. Recall those things that have been successfully for you and continue them. Discover those things you need to improve on and take action to make improvements. Avoid those things and people that have been detrimental to you and seek to understand why you have continued to allow yourself to fall prey to them repeatedly. If your damaging events are too overwhelming for you, you need to seek professional help. Some people do not seek help because they are ashamed to do so because they think it makes them weak or look crazy; however, what is crazy is that they continue to put themselves in one dangerous situation after another. Many times people put things so far behind them in their minds they forget. They then put their selves right back in the same situations. I know a person who did so and all I could hear their mother say is "the past is the past, and you just need to leave things in the past". Their reality was that their past kept being their present. Every six months to a year, they were back at the same crazy place in life year after year until they finally woke up.

You must simply love yourself and put your best self forward. In my book, *Anticipation – 10 Keys to Turning your Dreams into Reality*, I talk about self-love being one of the greatest loves of all. To share something with someone, you must first possess it yourself; therefore, if you do not love yourself, you cannot share that love with someone else. People who are bitter and hateful toward others, often are unsatisfied with their selves. You should learn to love the person that you are and "just do you". Always be Be-YOU-tiful. The "Fabulous Life" is when you have the "freedom of choice" to live life on your terms and enjoy the things YOU desire.

In loving yourself, you should not continually subject yourself to physical or emotional abuse. If it happens more than once, it is not them, it is you. What starts out as little angry outburst can something leads to devastating events. What starts out as boys or girls' night out every other night can often result in isolation and neglect. If you have spent the last two new year's eve in front of the television alone watching "___" rocking new year's eve to celebrate the coming in of the new year and your mate does not work the night shift, you should not care what is wrong with them. The holiday or event does not matter because "alone" is the key word. You should focus on what is wrong with you to continue to allow this to happen to you repeatedly. The phrase "turning the other cheek" does not mean for you to stay in neglectful or abusive situations. Stop being someone's victim. You can be a victim or a victor. The choice is yours. You should always behold yourself beautiful, believe, and understand you deserve better and just choose "better" and do you. Also, regardless of the obstacles and challenges you have had in your life, you should always move on and choose "Better over Bitter". Just learn how not to make the same mistakes repeatedly. It makes you a better you.

In "just doing you", you should have something to bring to the table beside drama. Investing in yourself will be one of the best returns on investments that you will ever make in your life. I am sure Visionary knew he had to have the foresight to acquire the skills needed to lay bricks or hire someone who did to do so. I heard it said that *"a beautiful face attracts a flirter, a beautiful heart attracts a lover, but beautiful character attracts a real man or woman"*. Four excellent traits for anyone to have are to be loving, self-sufficient, secure, and confident. Including Godly, these were the top things on my wish list for a real man. We have already talked about loving yourself so that you will be a loving person and be able to share that love with others. Now, let us speak of self-sufficiency, confidence and being secure. We all know that self-sufficiency is the ability to take care of your basic needs without outside help. If you do not have the education, skills or job to do so, you need to obtain them. When you can take care of yourself, no one can hold you in bondage unless you allow them. A confident person believes in themselves, knows what they want and goes after it, and adapts to situations with ease or can quickly size up a person or situation. They are usually positive people, and determined and hardworking. An insecure person lacks confidence and is too afraid they are not good enough. Self-sufficiency and confidence are more for you than the other person. People who are self-sufficient and confident tend to make better decisions and choices in life. The "glitz" does not usually blind them, and they can recognize unhealthy situations when they see them. You cannot be a penny looking for a dollar. I like to refer to them as "posers". Unless a penny is what the other person wants, this may pose a real problem for you. Some people do seek pennies; however, they are usually insecure and need someone they see as "less" to boost their egos which they can control. If you are self-sufficient and confident, you will be secure. You should always seek to make you the best you, you can be. I am a firm believer that if you are your best self, like moths to a fire or light, real love for you will find you. This is because you will shine bright like the stars in the night sky, and you will not have to go looking for love in the darkness of all the wrong places.

Do not make your quest to find someone else the center of your life. Seeking love should not be your primary goal. If love finds you, that is all good. In the meantime, prepare yourself, work hard and get out there and simply have fun living your best life. Participate in those things you like to do. Make your outings a quest to find yourself. Try new things that will enhance you as a person while you are having a blast. The best thing about a woman or man in any outfit should the person wearing the outfit and not the outfit itself; therefore, you should outfit your best self well. In outfitting yourself, you should live life on your terms and not someone else's terms. After all, it's your life.

*Opportunity has to have a reason to come knocking at your door.*

## 2:3 Be Approachable

Now that you have worked on yourself let's talk about approachability. You will never find, enjoy or keep anyone if you are not approachable. I cannot count the numerous times I have heard people say they are waiting on God to send them someone; yet, they cannot be approached. Well, maybe he/she has been trying. Some of these people are well into their fifties, and they have been singing the same tune for decades. Remember I said you will attract people based on who they perceive you to be. If you are unapproachable, you will be perceived as being boring, rude, too abrasive, unhappy, and unavailable. The following are my top suggestions that will make you more approachable:

1. **Get Out of Your Home.** Here is a concept that is a no-brainer. People can't approach you if they never see you or know you exist. Opportunity has to have a reason to knock on your door.

2. **Watch Your Body Language.** Body language makes up the majority part of communication. Your body language needs to be open. People approach people who they perceive to be friendly, open, and happy. Hold your head up, make eye contact, uncross your arms and smile. When you hold your head down, do not make eye contact, keep your arms crossed and do not smile, people cannot see your eyes, feel the warmth of your smile, and your arms are not welcoming as you greet people with open arms. Joseph Addison once said, *"What sunshine is to flowers, smiles are to humanity. They are but trifles, to be sure; but scattered along life's pathway, the good they do is inconceivable"*. A smile has a way of making the sun rise in your eyes and like moths to a flame; people will flock to this light. Often it is a reflection of an individual's heart. It has been my experience that these things are the majority of reasons people get approached. It shows that you are friendly and want someone to approach you. Also, remember not to wear sunglasses inside or outside if the light and sun are not shining too bright. People need to see your eyes.

3. **Look Good.** Attractiveness is approachable. I am not solely talking about looks because beauty is in the eye of the beholder. You just need to behold yourself beautiful, and your actions need to reflect it. People look good when they smile *(provided they have seen a dentist regularly)* are well groomed, have good hygiene, and their fashion is current.

4. **Isolate Yourself in Social Settings.** Sometimes people will not approach if you are among too many people. Isolate yourself from the group by taking a trip to the bathroom or somewhere else in the room. The other person will now have an opportunity to approach you. It is safe and OK to have one friend accompany you; however, a large group is unadvisable.

5. **Don't Be Rude.** There is nothing people hate worse than people who are rude to others; especially in public. Always be aware that people can see and hear you when you are talking to your friends, the waitress, waiter or clerk. Do you think they want to approach someone with such a nasty disposition? If you are rude to others, they feel that you will or might be rude to them or their friends and family as well.

6. **Beware of the Tone of Your Voice.** Make sure you are not always speaking in a loud and abrasive tone. People think it is a big turn off.

7. **Have a Conversation and Not a Sermon.** You need to save sermons for the pulpit. Unless you are doing mission work or you know the person's soul needs saving, when someone approaches you and say, "hello" unless you want to turn them off maybe your first response should not be "Where will you spend eternity, heaven or hell?" People talk, the word will get out that you just want an opportunity to preach. If you are a spiritual person, you do need to know if the two of you are spiritually compatible; however, this needs to occur later in conversation form and not a sermon. At this point, they are just speaking. Sometimes when people speak they don't actual want a discussion. They are only polite.

8. **Avoid Hanging Out with the Opposite Sex Too Much.** Don't expect the opposite sex to approach you if you are always hanging around too many of your opposite sex. For example, if you are a woman and you hang around a group of guys all the time, one of two things will probably happen: (1) either they will consider you as one of the guys or (2) one of the guys will lie and say that you are his woman or worse his jump off. Unless he is looking for a jump off type chick and you want to be one, you will not be perceived as a potential for "the one".

9. **Approach Others.** Sometimes you need to be a little bold. Show them that you are interested. Sometimes people are simply afraid especially if they perceive you to be out of their league. If they have not approached you yet, try approaching them, and if they are interested, they will take the bait. There is nothing wrong with you smiling and saying hello even if it is when you ask to borrow the ketchup *(which condiment does not matter)* from their table.

If you are not approachable, you can forget about the rest of the key ingredients in this book. You can be your best self, but if you are not approachable, no one will ever get the opportunity to know it.

Get to know who the person really is and if you can handle the type of relationship they will bring to the table; otherwise, you might wake up in the middle of a nightmare trying to figure out how to get out or cope.

## 2:4  Get to Know the Other Person

Once you have learned to love and be your best self and are approachable, you should get to know the other person. Getting to know the other person will also be part of your foundation in your "House of Love". This brings me back to the foolishness that "you must think like a man or woman". For me, the real problem with thinking like "a man" or "a woman" is you not knowing which man or woman to think like. My husband does not act like any other man I know or have known. From a common sense perspective, the key is not to just think like "a man" or "a woman" but to get to know the other person. Although you can generalize, people are different. You must always get to know the man or woman. This is the only way you will learn their likes and dislikes, what turns them on or off, what they really want out of a relationship, or if they are right for you. They may just be right for someone else.

How much time is enough? That would depend on what we are talking about. I am going to say for a serious relationship as in marriage anything before a year is too soon. You cannot rush into marriage or serious relationships. Anyone can fool anyone for a couple of months. While you can generally officially date or call someone girlfriend or boyfriend within a few months, the length of time for marriage should be longer. It's called an engagement. Marriage is or should be serious business as it has legal consequences. It took Visionary a long time to build his house made of bricks. Much longer than Lazy and Mediocre and they were eaten by the big bad wolf. You must put in enough time to get to know who the person is and if you can handle or want to deal with the type of relationship the other person will bring to the table. If you do not, you may wake up one day down the road in the middle of a nightmare trying to figure out how to either get out or cope. You will never understand who a person really is or what they really want out of a relationship unless you get to know them. Also, the consequences of intimacy and sex with people you do not know can be devastating. If you get to know them and discover they are not whom you thought, they were, or you do not want to deal with their world of drama it will be easier to walk away than to commit and then try to get out of it later. Now, if it has been more than several years, just move on.  It is disheartening to me to see someone who has been in a relationship for years when his or her significant other meets someone else, turns around and marries the other person within a year or less.

In getting to know the other person before you enter into a marriage or serious relationship, you must know the answers to and be on the same page to the following questions to start:

❖ Are either of you already in a serious relationship or marriage? If the answer is "yes", there is no need to finish this list at this point as it relates to the person in question.

❖ Where will you live?  If you both already have a property, on which property will be you live or will you sell and start out new?

❖ If you are religious, what religion will you follow and church will you attend?

❖ Where will you spend holidays. In some relationships, one mate forces the other to give up family celebration yearly as opposed to alternating.

❖ Will you have children, when, how many and how will they be raised, educated and disciplined?  In some cases, how many children do you already have?  One young man told me he had met this very attractive girl on a college campus who he started seeing.  When he finally went to her mother's house he learned that not only was she not in college, she had four children.  He realized the situation was not right for him and kept it moving.

❖ How will you respond to close relatives who will be your in-laws? Many of couples have let their relatives ruin their relationships. If they are willing to allow that to happen, they are not right for you.

❖ Will there be a prenuptial agreement?  You will be surprised at the people who only marry people for money and then seek to divorce them for half after a certain time limit has passed; especially in community property states in the United States.

❖ How much debt will each of you bring into the relationship, what are your plans to reduce it, and how do you feel about making future purchases on credit?

❖ Who will manage the household budget, make sure all the bills are paid, and write the checks?  Finances are among the top reasons relationship break up.

❖ Do either of you see sex as only a duty or how do each of you feel about intimacy?  This makes a big difference in a marriage.

❖ Does your mate want you to work outside the home after getting married or do you want to work outside the home once you are married?  Unless one of you is very wealthy, one income means fewer finances to work with.  How will you as a couple make financial decisions?

❖ What do you expect from each other?

❖ Are there any major illnesses?

❖ Did he or she leave their last mate because they became ill or lost their job?  I know far too many couples in serious relationships and married couples whose significant other left them when they became ill or lost their high paying job.  Marriage is supposed to be for better or worse; however, some people treat worse as an opportunity to leave.

The last bullet hits home with me.  After I had finished my last book and this book, I diagnosed with breast cancer while I was out on leave because of work-related injuries and had to have surgery. Although I had valid work excuses, in the same month I was diagnosed with breast cancer, I lost my job and had to seek legal remedies for Title VII Civil Rights violations under the ADA and Rehabilitation Acts. Regardless of my situation, my husband has been right there by my side to help me explore these legal options and to care for me. When I had my surgery, I could barely do anything for myself. My husband stepped up to the plate and filled in the gaps. Just as I did after he could not walk for a period time from complication of a fall off a ship's latter onto the deck floor. We have come a long way through our bitter storms together and although it is not over yet, I am at ease going forward. If you are reading this and cannot relate because you have never experienced any personal storms, just keep living. It took our storm years to come. My faith, my will, my husband, my family, and my true friends have kept me going. My blessings are many and I am so grateful. This is one of the reasons it is so very important to get to know people before you jump into long-term relationships. When you go through something, you will find out who your true love and friends really are by their actions. Many times the signs have always been there, we just never paid any attention to them. Some of the people that have finally shown their true colors are the same people they have always been. Seek to surround yourself with goodness and virtue and happiness will always follow. Some may think that these are judgmental approaches to life; however, it would depend on your goals in life. Are you trying to be popular or are you trying to live a healthy lifestyle? Popularity and a healthy lifestyle do not necessarily go hand in hand. It is much easier to live a healthy lifestyle than it is to "stay" popular. People that can "make it rain" downpours find themselves very popular at times; however, the minute their downpour turns into a drizzle or their ability to "make it rain" stops often their relevance to their current crowd or mate decreases.

You may have your questions to add to the list relevant to you, but the above is a good start. Whether it is "looking before jumping the broom" or looking before you jump into something that is tough to get out of, you just must look before you jump. It goes back to building that DREAMTEAM I spoke about in my book, "Anticipation, 10 Keys to Turning Your Dreams into Reality". Make your realities healthy by getting to know people and carefully choosing whom you allow in or to remain in your circle. Removing the wrong people from your circle is not hating them. It is loving yourself enough to understand that you need to surround yourself with uplifting, positive people. You should never be the smartest person on your DREAMTEAM. If no one is smarter than you in your circle, how will you ever grow? It is why you should always surround yourself with greatness. You must rid all other negativities from your space. Make sure you stay away from what I call the "Valley of the Nays": *Nay Seers* as they will never see your vision, *Nay Doers* as they will never contribute, and *Naysayers* as they only know negativity. It will make your life's journey easier.

*In the real estate of life, it's all about the situation.*
*You must learn to recognize and choose situations*
*that are compatible with your lifestyle to aide in the*
*blending of two into one.*

## 2:5 Recognize Dysfunction and Choose the Right Situation

Getting to know a person, learning to recognize dysfunction, and choosing the right situation should all go hand and hand. Again, this book is not meant to be judgmental. It is about minimizing the risk factors common in relationship failure. Hence, your life is yours, and you should be able to live it the way you desire on your terms and not the way someone else dictates to you by trying to make you feel guilty for wanting something better in life. Yes, you will be called names just like I was called names. Some of them very hurtful but it is in your best interest to hold fast to your convictions. It is more about people learning to recognize situations that are compatible with their lifestyle to aid in the blending of two into one. Remember it is all about "Location, Location, and Location" or, in this case, the right "Situation, Situation, Situation" as in the environment. As I said at the beginning of this book, there is no such thing as a "perfect" person; therefore, there is no such thing as a perfect family. However, usually, in an ideal family situation parents and adult children understand their issues and work together to solve them as opposed to family members who are in denial and believe that their situation is normal and not a real problem. Remember what happened to Lazy, who was in denial. In these cases, family members *(Mediocre)* sometimes uphold and accommodate one sibling or parent in their hurtful behavior. The keys are denial and the perception of normal that sometimes continue through generations. How will you and your mate understand each other if you cannot relate to each other?

Have you ever thought that you found the right person, only to learn that their life is jacked up? If you use the proper term, it is dysfunctional. People are often in denial regarding their actual situation. If the individual has a crazy ex that acts like he or she is from Satan's den or other family members not too far from there, it is best that you keep it moving. If you do not, you may spend a lifetime trying to get people to understand you who simply cannot. They usually see their situation as normal; therefore, they will never see you as normal unless your lifestyle starts to mimic their way of life. When you allow others to stop you, you become just like them. Your goal should not be to become like them. Chances are they will only see you as someone who thinks they are better than others; however, you should know that you make better choices than the average "crackhead." If not, you need to go back to the essential element of "Loving and Be Your Best Self" before you attempt to find anyone else. It does not matter if you are the CEO of a Fortune 500 company; they will likely see you as nothing. You will probably always have that "everything that glitters it not gold effect". You will never have control of these situations and usually, neither will your mate. There is usually no respect for the partner; therefore, you cannot expect any respect for yourself either. If your mate does not have the courage to stand up to outside interference, dysfunctional and toxic situations will fill your relationship regularly. These conditions often become too stressful to handle.

Dysfunctional and toxic situations can lead to serious health problems down the road if you cannot weather the storms continuously over the course of years. Especially if your mate is not in control of their situation or does not have the ability to keep negative/toxic people out of their business and simply love them from a distance. Studies have shown that stress lowers one's immune system. Your immune system is essentially your defense mechanism to fight off diseases. Just look around you, how many people do you know that have been in dysfunctional and toxic relationships that are now ill? I know some horror stories, some that have led to death, physically or even mentally.

How does one recognize dysfunctional behavior? Recognizing dysfunction can be very hard to do if you have been surrounded by this behavior your entire life. People who have had no role model of a healthy relationship will not be able to recognize one. I am familiar with some aspects as I spent eight years of my professional career and five years of my volunteer career working with youth organizations assisting leaders to recognize dysfunction and child abuse and providing community resources for reporting and assistance. First, let us look at what a few experts *(Dr. Stoop and Masteller and Dr. Kaslow)* have had to say about dysfunction as it relates to family. According to Wikipedia, the doctors have said the following:

- A dysfunctional family is a family in which conflict, misbehavior, and often child neglect or abuse on the part of individual parents occur continually and regularly, leading other members to accommodate such actions. Children sometimes grow up in such families with the understanding that such an arrangement is normal.

- Dysfunctional family members have common features and behavior patterns as a result of their experiences within the family structure. This tends to reinforce the dysfunctional behavior, either through enabling or perpetuation.

Some features are common to most dysfunctional families:

- Lack of empathy, understanding, and sensitivity towards certain family members, while expressing extreme empathy towards one or more members *(or even pets)* that have real or perceived "special needs." In other words, one family member continuously receives far more than he or she deserves, while another is marginalized.

- Denial *(refusal to acknowledge abusive behavior, possibly believing that the situation is normal or even beneficial; also known as the "elephant in the room.")*

- Inadequate or missing boundaries for self *(e.g. tolerating inappropriate treatment from others, failing to express what is acceptable and unacceptable treatment, tolerance of physical, emotional or sexual abuse.)*

- Disrespect of others' boundaries *(e.g. physical contact that other person dislikes; breaking important promises without just cause; purposefully violating a boundary another person has expressed)*

- Extremes in conflict *(either too much fighting or insufficient peaceful arguing between family members)*

- Unequal or unfair treatment of one or more family members due to their birth order, gender, age, family role *(mother, etc.)*, abilities, race, caste, etc. *(may include frequent appeasement of one)*

You cannot determine dysfunction by the cover of people. It knows no race, social, financial or intellectual boundaries. When children grow up in dysfunctional families, often they go on to become someone's mate. If they do not receive positive outside intervention, they usually continue this cycle of dysfunction for generations. If you are in this type of situation, it is never too late to break the cycle. Professional help is available if needed. The following are a few real world scenarios of dysfunctional and toxic situations:

Situation #1, The Postman Delivers Often
*Crazy Love:*

You meet a young man and he already have one or two kids by different women, and another one on the way or you meet an old man, and he has a family over here and a family over there, and sometimes he has never been married to any of the mothers. You then come to find out that the men are father and son. Now do you see the generational pattern? Unless they are multi-millionaires, and you only are just trying to get paid, just run! This one should be common sense and is not worth discussing in detail. However, you must also realize that wells sometimes run dry, and the postage/costs are usually too heavy of a burden to bear for a lifetime. You will be so busy trying to help pay child support, or you will end up having to take care of any kids you may have together on your own, or this is a pattern. You may be the next "baby mama" on the list and still end up taking care of your kids on your own. Some will think I am off base with this one; however, have you ever seen the dramatic talk shows that are on television that deals with DNA testing. These shows often contain this type of man. Now, do you get the point? The obituary of this sort of man's funeral is usually a book, or the print is so small you can hardly read it as all the children's names often can't fit on a half fold sheet of standard size paper. I have seen obituaries where some men have had as many as eighteen to twenty kids by various women. Part of the time, most of these men do not even remember sleeping with some of the women. Who is considering the children in all these situations? This type of situation is dominant in some cultures and both men and women except it. They refer to it as "a man is going to be a man" or "he's just out doing his thang." You should want better for yourself, your daughters, your sons or your grandchildren. It is also a dangerous lifestyle. Case in point: I know at least four people who have died of AIDS. Three from mates who were "hitting" everything they could then coming home and sleeping with their partners and the other from drug use who was also sleeping with other people. Again, this is not judgmental; it is real facts of life regarding choices and their consequences. You only get one life, and it is in your best interest to limit your risks if you want to stick around as long as you can. I like and enjoy sex in my marriage as much as the next person, but I was never willing to die for it. Someone told me the other month where they work with youth, a young lady came to the center that was only 18 or 19 who already had five kids by five different males. That is going to be a difficult journey to travel. You must have enough common sense to wait for the right person for you to marry and, believe me; the right person for you does exist. You just need to be ready when they come along.

Situation #2, The Good, The Bad, & The Ugly
*Dangerous Love:*

There once was one of the most beautiful woman I had ever seen as a child. She was seen a good throughout her circle and beyond. She married a gorgeous man with horrible behavior I felt, and they had two beautiful girls together. No matter how good their situation could have ever been, the bad and the ugly soon showed up, took over and ruled. Her husband often abused her both mentally and physically on a daily basis. In this family abuse was normal. The abuse led to him shooting her; however, she did not die from the shooting. After a period, she started to get sick and with each sickness, it began to get harder and harder for her to recover. She eventually died from cancer. She simply did not have the strength, mentally or physically, to fight for her life. The social isolation did not help either. However, as the good book says, you reap what you sow. The story is that he was on the down low, and some years later, he was robbed and beaten half to death and stuffed in the truck of his car. He never quite recovered and later died from complications of AIDS. You just cannot put negative energy into the universe and expect it not to show back up on your doorsteps eventually. No one needs this type of situation. If you are in this type of situation, you need to seek help immediately before it is too late for you.

Situation #3, The Big House in Big Daddy's World
*Foolish Love:*

Nice car, nice money, nice crib and nice digs and you're just the one Big Daddy is looking for, for his next gig. You see Big Daddy has many gigs, and it just depends where you will fall on his pyramid scheme of love. You may think you are fortunate if you manage to reach the top of big daddy's pyramid and make it into the "Big House" because of all the others you are above; however, the big house is a very lonely place in Big Daddy's world even when he is there. I call the house in Big Daddy's World "big" mainly because there are "big" problems in Big Daddy's World that mainly you will have to bare. Making it to the Big House is how Big Daddy defines love, as he will often tell. There you will find plenty to do and plenty of free time to do it as well. Maybe you think you will last longer in the Big House than the last gig did or some may view themselves as lucky if they land at the bottom of Big Daddy pyramid because they think that just like Big Daddy boots right now he also has a lot of loot. Could it be that Big Daddy sent you an invitation to the big house because you are the one he thinks has the loot? Big Daddy and material possession *(including you)* will go hand and hand. There will be nothing left but to survive in Big Daddy's world if you can. On the outside looking in everything looks great, but it will be the loneliness and the absence of real love that you will eventually come to hate. There are a lot of "Big Daddies" and "Big Mamas" in this world. If you can manage to avoid, you will not fill your life with a void.

Scenario #4, Bad Boys Rock
*Toxic Love:*

The "bad boy" type attract many women. Their personas are usually exciting and attractive to these women. Many times, these women grew up as "good girls" and always thought they were missing the excitement in their life. However, when the women usually fall victim to these bad boys and the crowd they hang around, their life and sometimes their children's life eventually becomes fatal. Too many people have had to bury their relatives behind this type of love. I knew someone who fell victim to this kind of situation. Her family will forever miss them. It is unfortunate that you can find this type of love all over this country and beyond. I had goggled to see what the national news was saying about her situation and forgot, to put her name and city, and I was shocked. If this is the type of mate that you are always falling for, maybe you need to reevaluate yourself first before it is too late for you.


Scenario #5, Too Educated to Quit
*Ignorant Love:*

Ms. Independent can usually answer every question known to man from any book, but cannot explain why in the wrong places for a mate and love she continues to look. She has many degrees, and that is a known fact, but good common sense she always seems to lack. Somehow she thinks the wrong men *(abusers, criminals, gamblers, leeches & players)* are good catches. She is always searching for inappropriate matches. Her life is filled with so much stress. Her mates have put her through too many test. Her health is now not at its best. Let us just face it, education without common sense is nonsense. While someone can stay in this type of relationship for a long time, it usually is a nightmare and comes with a lot of heartache and pain over the years.

Scenario #6, The Girl Next Door
*Naïve Love:*

There once was this girl next door who lived on the outskirts of a small town in the country sheltered from many ways of the world. It was unbelievable how just thirty to forty minutes away from the big city in the same state could make a big difference in someone's experiences. Although she was an attractive young lady, she was a bit of a tomboy who played basketball, softball, and ran track. Her best friends where mostly guys whom she never dated but everybody else wanted to date; therefore, beyond her relatives, she was not real popular with the girls. She had grown up playing basketball and kickball with her brother and the boys in the neighborhood. They always had an odd number of them and from small kids they always needed another player, and she was it. She was more like their sister than anything else. When she was a teenager in high school about 15 years of age, she met a young man who had come to one of her basketball games with her bus driver's son from two cities over. She did not see him again until two years later when she was with one of her friend guys who turned out to be one of his best friends. They began to date, and he would become her first love. She thought the sun rose and set in him. Their relationship started off magical as they never argued or fought and he was always kind and good to her. They could talk about anything until they both would fall asleep on the phone in the wee hours of the morning. She would even talk on the phone with his mother. One day out of the blue the young man called her and told her it was over. His actions caught her off guard. She was shocked. He told her that his best friend had told him that he and she had done all types of sex acts and that he could not get over it. She told him that his best friend was lying and asked him why now did he bring this back up after so much time had passed and it was he who initially told her that he knew that she and his friend never dated or had a sex the night he asked for her phone number.

After they had talked on the phone for the very first time after exchanging numbers, the young lady had told him what happened to his friend and her friendship which was now over after his friend had tried to force his self on her. He had asked her for her panties, and she said no, and he decided he was going to take them. This event took place after she had told their mutual friend guy that she had already met the young man before and thought he was very handsome then and she would like to get to know him better, and they had exchanged phone numbers. The guy seemed to be upset and told her he did not want her to call his friend. The young lady did not know at the time that he had told all his boys she was his girl. The guy then told her he needed to stop by a friend's place who was a cop first, but when they got there, no one was home, and he did attempt to try something, but she locked herself in the bathroom and would not come out until the friend came home 15 minutes later. It was a setup as the cop was the handsome young man's older brother and the friend guy just wanted the policeman to see him with her. He made her so mad that she demanded to go back to her car now and at one point got out of the car and started walking down a dark street. He told her he was not going to bother her anymore, but he could not leave her on the street in the dark walking at night. She told him that night she no longer considered him as a friend and he told her he was not going to allow her to date his friend. The truth was that the young lady had no attraction for the mutual friend guy at all, never kissed the friend and only went to play video games with him after he bugged her about the fact that they were friends but she would never be seen in public with him because she thought he was ugly. She had always had other friend guys all her life who she went numerous places with even their homes and shopping who never tried anything with her. She was always just like one of the guys. Now, she considered him to be the ugliest person in the world. She now understood that he was a wolf in sheep clothing who only asked her to go play video games so that people could see them together. It is why he made the extra stops along the way. Turns out the guy had lied to his friends and told them they were in a relationship, and he was embarrassed when she told them they were not and after that night his friend and the young lady were now dating and seemed to like each other a lot. Remember she already had a crush on the young man from two years prior but did not know if he remembered her as she now looked very different. She had gone from tomboy to model and had great fashion sense. How she became a model is that when she was shopping for school clothes her first year of college she went to this store and was trying on clothes and someone from a modeling agency had come in to pick up some clothes for a fashion show. When she came out of the dressing room to get a sales clerk assistance they noticed her and told her they thought she would make a good model as she had the body and bone structure for it. Turns out they were right. They sent her to training, and the camera seemed to love her. She learned very quickly, and she could walk the runway. Gone were the days of tomboyish attire. When she entered college, no one could have guessed she used to be a tomboy. Then she met the young man's best friend who she never liked as anything more than a friend.

The young lady refused to fight with the young man who she had fallen in love with about the issue. She always felt like her grandmother once told her that if it is true love and you let it go, it would always find its way back. Also, she had always been taught not to go looking for trouble. However, looking back, she did not understand how he could have even thought that those lies were true because if she did not know how to do all those things his best friend mentioned with him how could she have done them before him. They broke up and had no contact for a year or so or more. The young lady who had graduated from a community college transferred to a senior college that spring, continued to model, and started working a full-time job to assist with the expense. She began to date a college football player who turned professional. She and the football player had a good relationship, but there was one major problem. He had a child by a girl his freshman year of college. He asked the young lady for them not to show any affections toward each other when they were around his son. The child would just freak out if anyone touched his dad as he had this notion in his head that his father was going to get back with his mother. The young lady felt that she was too young for this type of drama. She and the football player broke up and became good friends. Well, that Christmas her first love tracked her down while she was visiting her grandmother and told her that he had missed her and just wanted to talk. They talked about what they had been doing since they were last together.

The young lady spoke the truth; however, unknown to her, the young man did not tell the truth. Over the next weeks, they decided to get back together. The first person, the young lady, told was his mother when she answered the phone after she called him one day but there was a big secret that even the mother did not tell the young lady. His brother, the cop, knew the secret but did not tell as well. Her so called friends said they were asked not to say anything to her. The young lady trusted him and was so busy with college and modeling until she never took the time to look or check anything out. To make a long story short, trouble found her. She went to a Christmas party one year and caught the attention of an eligible, handsome guy who had come home for the holidays. He was interested in her. When he inquired as to who she was, he was told that she was unavailable as she was the girlfriend of the cop's brother. The eligible guy revealed to the young lady's friend at the party that he thought the cop's brother had gotten married, but he had been out of town for a while and wasn't quite sure if they were still together or married. That particular friend told the young lady and the next day they checked the court records to find out. It turns out that the year they were broken up he did get married but had now filed for a divorce. There was another big secret as well, she found out he had a child. The young lady asked to meet him in the park and confronted him with the truth. He told her he knew she would never agree to see him again if she knew the truth because she had told him about the football player and that is why he lied and asked others not to tell. He told her how violent his situation had become which his best friend backed up, and he had the scars to show. The young lady felt sorry for him as she never understood violence. However, it was now clear to her why some people were looking at her funny. Her reputation would again suffer a major blow from all ends. Even the friend that told her the big secret used it against her when her mother was asking her why can't she be more like the young lady. The friend told her mother, "At least I never got involved with someone that was married". From that point forward the friend's mom and her sister would make remarks about the young lady in her presence. They did so because the aunt's husband had left her for another woman. It did not matter that the young lady never knew the young man had gotten married or had a child. It did not matter that the young lady was not the cause of their breakup. Her name in the streets was now tarnished.

Gone were the days of thinking guys only wanted to be her friend even when they told her that is all they wanted. Also, gone were the days of thinking everything a man tells you is the truth. Now her reputation had gone from the girl next door to something very different even though it was all a lie. It was very hurtful to her. The cop certainly never let her live it down as he had started to try to date one of her friends and one time the ugly hearted man fell off a ladder, and the cop told the woman to tell the young lady. When her friend did the young lady said to her, *"and you are telling me because? I have said far too many times that he was only a friend guy once but not anymore, and I do not care what happens to him because you can forgive someone (even though the man never asked anyone to forgive him) but there does not have to be reconciliation. His intent was evil. He intentionally told lies that he knew would ruin my reputation, and that is what he was trying to do. Is he supposed to get some reward for it? He got what he wanted in the end. His best friend and I are not dating anymore, and he is no longer one of my friends. I do not think about him as my mind does don't need any negative energy in its space. So unless you are trying to tell me that "negative energy" has left the earth, I do not want to hear anything about him"*. Negative energy is the same reason she had to leave some of her so called girlfriends she had met after graduating high school alone. They were too negative and always made negative comments about how she was skinny. They made her feel bad when guys wanted to dance with or talk to her as opposed to them. Most of them had big butts and chest when they were young. That was their greatest assets. Again, too much negative energy in her space. Her self-esteem improved significantly afterward.

You can't be naïve in life. You must understand that some people will lie to you just to be with you. You cannot listen to others tell you that you shouldn't go looking for trouble. You must check out your situation before it checks you out.

Scenario #7, Satan Wears Red
*Manipulative and Dysfunctional Family Love:*

There was a man who met a woman who was dating his brother. The brother had come to live with him *(a true player that was living "the life" at the time)*. Eventually, the brother dropped the woman. After all, game does recognize game. The woman who already had a child by another man then set her sights on a bigger prize, the government man *(G-man)*. He said she started by offering to babysit his child by his wife who had previously cheated on him and had fallen victim to drugs. The G-man saw this as kind, and the goodness in him thought that she was kind at heart as well. He could not see through all the manipulation. The G-man starts a relationship with her and discovers she is pregnant. He says he had doubts about if the child was his child. The woman has the child, yet the G-man fails to ask for a blood test. Even though he had doubts, he divorces his wife who is on drugs and marries the woman in pure shotgun fashion as he had decided to relocate to another state but the woman and her father had different ideas. He marries her. It turns out that there was a rumor that the woman tried to stab the pregnant wife of a man she was involved with, and she was involved with drugs also. After approximately two months of marriage, he goes away on an extended business trip leaving his son from a previous marriage in her care. While he was away, his mother went to visit the new wife. The wife had another man living in the G-man's home. She told the G-man's mother that the man was a friend of her son and that he had asked him to keep an eye on them while he was gone. The G-man returned six to nine months later only to find that another man had been living in his home. The wife had the kids calling the man uncle. The G-man had to leave his home as he had nowhere to stay anymore. In a very sick twist, the G-man who had befriended the man would stay there to get to see his son that the woman would not return to him. Eventually, he found a place to live and when he went to get his son, she would not give him the child's clothes or things and he had to purchase new clothes for the child to wear. She continued to cohabitate with the man she moved into the G-man's home and had a kid with him. The G-man says that the woman told him that she was going through medical problems, and she asked that he not divorce her so that she can keep medical benefits. After a while, he figured out all of what was told to him was not true and filed for a divorce. She then had a lawyer file a response petition to assert paternity issues regarding the child she had by the man she moved into the G-man's home and maternity issues regarding the G-man's son from his previous marriage. The divorce went on for a lengthy time. In so many words, the petition stated that the baby she had with the man she moved into the G-man's home should be considered a child of the marriage because the child was born while she was still legally married to the G-man and the child believed the G-man was his father. The argument is a bazaar argument since the woman had been living with the man she moved into the home. She had put his name on the birth certificate, and the child knew him to be his father. The court ordered blood test through the DA's office that the G-man had to pay for came back in real Maury Povich fashion, "You Are Not the Father"! As if anyone ever doubted that, the test would come back any other way. The child knew his father was not the G-man. While all this was going on some of the G-man's family was eating her up as if she was the best thing since water and running around the countryside talking about how she was a good wife and mother and the G-man and her were going to get back together.

Also, she then asked for attorney fees for these unreasonable positions *(lies)* she asserted. While the courts sorted out the truth, the G-man in mediation foolishly agreed to allow his son to return to her home. He was due to leave for another government business trip and the child when asked told the court he wanted to stay there with the other kids. The boy later said he was afraid what the woman would do to him if he told the truth. The child later said the woman had knocked him out with a punch after he tried to send his dad a letter telling him about the woman's abuse previously when he was away. The woman had the support of the G-man's two cousins and their mother. Also, the G-man's mother sent him a letter telling him what a great time she had with the woman and her family when they came to visit her for the holidays. The mother was referring to all the kids of the woman as being her grandchildren. The woman asked the military man for a Power-of-Attorney to take care of business on the child's behalf. The military man said his mother had always taught him to turn the other cheek. The mother and other relatives were still dealing with the woman. He thought the relationship which had always been violent was now civil. He even told people how polite/friendly it was now. The G-man left for duty. When he did, the woman filed for welfare assistance saying that the G-man had deserted the child, and she did not know where he was living. She knew that he was on government duty, and she was receiving money for the child's care while he was away. She proceeded to get rid of most of the G-man's possessions and gained access to his bank account and opened a new charge account in his name. At some point the son says that she began to have an affair with one of the G-man's cousin. After the woman heard the G-man had met someone, the woman started visiting the G-man's mother and started telling people in the G-man's family that they were getting back together. At some point, she had moved yet another man into her home. She went and had pictures made of her and the kids and sent them to various family members. The child says he was kicked out on the streets and had scars from where he says he was beaten with an extension cord. When the military man returned he discovered all his possessions was gone, he only had $14 in the bank. When he went to get his son like the court papers said he was to do when he returned, the woman hit him in the mouth and he called cops to help retrieve his son. Again, having to retrieve him without any clothes. The woman ran the account she opened in his name up to over a thousand dollars that she did not pay, and the state then filed a suit against him because they gave the woman financial assistance for his son. He finally won the case against the state after spending thousands of dollars in attorney fees to resolve the situation and his name. The child and the service member both suffered mental and physical abuse. Before the G-man left for duty, she even sought to get rid of anyone that came into the service man's life and mostly used or tried to use his family to do so. A point that the woman would frequently brag about to some. Her family foot soldiers as she referred to them were always willing to do her dirty work.

You see, the G-man who had been taught to forget about the past and forgive never learned and was never taught that forgiveness and reconciliation are two different things. Forgiveness only takes one person, but reconciliation takes two. There is nothing in the good book that says you must stay involved with toxic, abusive persons or situations. Forgiveness does not mean that you are supposed to forget or allow yourself to continue to be a victim. You have a responsibility to protect yourself and your children. People who are constant victims keep placing themselves around people whose intent is to hurt them in the first place. Forgiveness also does not mean that we cease to talk about or cover up the abuse. You must never protect abusers by your silence or made up stories. It only allows them to abuse again much easier. You should not trust people who knew you would be hurt but did not care. A lot of people feel this does not apply to family members; however, it does. Being related to someone does not give you a free "abuse at will" card. These are the people that are supposed to have your back and love you.

Even though the G-man man was going through a difficult time, spent thousands of dollars in litigation, and was emotionally and physically abused, he still did not receive the family support he should have gotten from some family members. There were some excellent family members in his family, but this dysfunctional scenario is not about those members. The scenario is about the bad, the fence-riders and the family members that continually put their selves in the middle only adding to the problem. The military man's son said in court documents and told family members that he was abused both physically and emotionally, exposed to drugs, and alienated from his father. Some of the service member's family upheld the woman in all her wrong doings and wanted him to take her back. They and the woman are still friends to this date. After the G-man had obtained the divorce, the foolishness continued for years and years. His new wife still feels the backlash from this dysfunction today.

Was this behavior bazaar and awful? Sure it was; however, crazy is as crazy does, and the same goes for dysfunction. Rather than deal with his family and tell them to stay out of his business from the very beginning he chose to stay away, ignore and allowed them to continue to interfere, which the woman used to aid in her cause. In what world would any of the above scenario have been functional? You might ask yourself, how could anyone identify with such and go against their flesh and blood? People often see something of themselves in others whether they are right or wrong. A new meaning to "birds of a feather flock together." Whether it was the manipulation, drugs, "party"/good time, sex, or the admiration of a single parent just trying to make it, it does not matter, it was wrong. This situation was dysfunctional and only very strong people could survive it. The G-man himself was in denial. There was nothing good about this situation only manipulations and lies. Satan had nothing on this woman.

Red is a very hard color stain to remove from the fabric of your life, and sometimes we meet people whose fabric of life is so stained, that it shines through the sheep clothing that they are wearing. Learn to recognize the wolf or devil in people early and keep it moving. It was unfortunate that the G-man did not recognize dysfunction and choose right from the beginning and thought that he could shelter anyone else from the manipulation and insanity. No one should expect protection from the wrath of this type of a dysfunctional situation. It does not matter how good you may be; dysfunction can overshadow you. Unless you can deal with being in a fight the majority of your life, it is best that you keep it moving. I know that I love my brother and sister enough that if someone did something like this to them, I would certainly not be partying or sitting around having a good time with them. My grandmother taught me this. I had an uncle that married to a woman who left him after X amount of years. She had two kids by my uncle and one by another man who had been sent to prison when the child was a baby. When her first child's father got out of jail, she divorced my uncle. My uncle had to sell everything he had worked for over the years in the divorce. My uncle's ex-wife never worked and when the money ran out from the divorce, the man, ex-con, left her. She phoned my grandmother and told her that my uncle would not let her use his airline passes so that she could bring her grandkids to visit her. My uncle worked for a major airline. My grandmother's stance was I know my son has visitation rights, he brings the kids to see me every year on his vacation, and they call me when they visit him. Please do not call here again. The truth was that my uncle's ex-wife had family in the same state my grandmother lived in, and it was a way for her to see them free. My uncle brought his kids to see not only my grandmother but, his ex's family and us as well when he visited. My uncle was a good man just like the G-man above. My grandmother telephoned her kids and requested that they not get involved in what she referred to as foolish nonsense. My family supported my uncle and my grandmother in their decisions, and we avoided all the manipulation and drama. Today those children now adults are just as close to our family as they are to their mother's family. Again, in healthy situations, family members usually recognize their issues and work together to solve them and do not become part of the problem.

Here is a tip for you when deciding to get serious about someone who travels for extended periods with their job. Make sure you visit the place where they live and not where they are stationed temporarily. It is especially hard if they are in the marines or navy as they are usually extremely mobile a great deal of the time. Check out what they say their realities are even if you have to look at court documents which you can find where they live. Government personnel represent a different kind of potential mate. Although they are good catches, they are targets. People prey on them just to reap the benefits being married to one brings. It rarely constitutes love on the predators' part. The government personnel are usually lonely and make easy prey. It is not rare for them to get married multiple times.

How much can you handle? I don't know the answer to that question in general. What I do know is that these situations are very stressful, and stress is contributing factor to illnesses. People are different and can handle different levels of stuff. But the common sense question is why? Why should you want to go through so much pain and suffering when you can have better? Life is all about choices. The better choices we make, the better life we and those we are responsible for can enjoy. It is up to you, and you can choose "the right situation". Do not make your dream a nightmare and be eaten by the "big bad wolf" of life.

In your real estate of life, it will be all about the "Situation, Situation, Situation". Remember I said earlier that there were no perfect places where you can find perfect people. However, some situations are more suitable for your lifestyle. Those are the ones you need to seek. You will find that you can cope with and fit into those situations better. It about making your journey through life as enjoyable and smooth as possible so you can focus on other goals in life. Negativity simply cannot be the mainstay of your life. It drains you of the energy and creativity needed for not only the necessary things in life but for turning your dreams into reality. The right action for you will be to choose the right situation for yourself and children if you have them.

Grant me the serenity to accept the fact that
I cannot change others,
The courage to change those things I can that
I want to see within myself,
And the wisdom to recognize with whom
my time is better spent that will make all the difference.

## 2:6　Choose the Right Mate for You

Once you have gotten to know the other person and their situation, you should choose the right mate for you. If you do not choose the right partner, none of the other essential ingredients will matter. You cannot have a house with a foundation alone. Every house also needs a proper structure to withstand the test of times. The right mate is the nail that will hold the structure and the mortar that will hold the bricks in your "House of Love" together. Trying to build a healthy relationship without the right mate is like attempting to make potato soup without the potatoes. Relationships are not that hard; however, being in a relationship with the wrong person is hard.

## Make A List

As previously suggested, make a list. The list can be a mental list, or if you have trouble remembering, you should write it down and refer to it periodically or as frequent as needed. If you meet someone, and you know that he or she do not possess any of the most important things on your list, don't waste time. You should keep it moving. Just like the four traits I mentioned in the "Love and Be Your Best Self" section of this book, that you should bring to the table, your mate needs to bring at least the same four traits to the table:

(1) Loving
(2) Self-Sufficient
(3) Confident
(4) Secure

You can add other traits to the list. I have included a form for you to use in the back of this book for your convenience to get you started. Another one on my list as mentioned earlier was that I wanted a man that was Godly. If these traits are not there, you cannot try to force them. You should never attempt to change a person, especially if they do not want to change. It only leads to misery. You cannot change other people. You can only change some of the things you want to see within yourself. You should always remember a modified version of the Serenity Prayer when it comes to change and come time to choose the right mate:

*Grant me the serenity to accept the fact that I cannot change others,*
*The courage to change those things I can that I want to see within myself,*
*And the wisdom to recognize with whom my time is better spent that will make all*
*the difference.*

We have all heard of making a list when it comes to something as essential as going to the grocery store to buy food. Advertisers have drilled this into our mental memory about making a list when we are going to make one of the most significant purchases in our lives of buying a home. You should treat finding the right mate as one of the most important investments you will make in your life. It will lead to your wellbeing and sanity. Life is stressful enough. You do not need to add to the stress by choosing wrong.

You should never base choosing the right mate on attraction and looks alone. Just because someone attracts you, it does not mean he or she are right for you especially if their lifestyle is in conflict with yours. Although attraction is helpful, it should not be the only factor. Looks do not make a person and looks tend to change or fade. Then, what are you going to do? Point in case: How many attractive people do you know right now that are in terrible relationships. Looks alone have never kept anyone in a relationship or anyone from cheating on someone with other people. Just look at Hollywood where some of the most beautiful women in the world exist. Cheating from their partners has become these women's nemeses. In addition, no one's skin color is an indication of a perfect mate. Beauty is not confined to certain skin colors. Crazy, ignorance and an ugly heart are universal and knows no color.

Just like attraction, money is also helpful; however, it too should not be the only factor. Just because a person has, money or access to money today does mean they will have money or access to it in the future. When the money runs out there has to be something left. Financial or money problems *(too little or even too much)* are one of the leading causes of breakups in relationships. People who have a love for each other can go through something or struggle together. Those who are only in it for the money, usually leave when the money runs out or soon after one of them in the relationship gets their own.

# Live Within Your Means

In choosing the right mate, you should select one that is willing to live within the two of your means. Too often, a lot of us are living far beyond our means. You should never risk the necessities. If one of you loses your job, the other's paycheck should be able to cover the house note including insurance and utilities. You really should keep at least six house and lease payments and living expenses in the bank or more. Unless you have paid for your house, you should not pay more for your car than your house note. Unless you are rich, maybe it is not such a good idea to get married, purchase a brand new house and buy two new cars all at the same time. Your clothing and accessory allowance should not be more than your house note. Does it make good common sense to spend five or more hundred dollars on an accessory when you do not have five or more hundred dollars in the bank?

The idea is to have a plan. To take care of the necessities each month, you must budget. Although your percentages will vary depending upon the two of your individual situation among the different categories, the following is a general list of the categories that should be on your budget:

Housing
> Mortgage or Rent

Property Taxes or HOA fees *(If you are purchasing or own your home)*
> Utilities

> Repairs *(If you are purchasing or own your home)*

> Food

Automobile
> Car Loan

> Fuel/Gas

> Repairs

Insurance
> Mortgage or Rental

> Health

> Life

> Automobile

Savings *(always allocate money for an emergency fund or reserves)*

Clothing

Entertainment

Miscellaneous

## Be Equally Yoked

You must be equally yoked. This is common sense. Opposites do attract; however, you and your mate must have more things in common than you do that are different. For example:

- If you are a Christian and your mate is an atheist, it will never work. When you are worshiping a higher being and they are worshiping something that you cannot, I do not care how good they look in those jeans, it is not likely to work. Get to know the other person's religious beliefs before you jump into a serious relationship or jump the broom *(Look before you Jump)*.

- If you are drug-free, and your mate is foolish enough to do drugs, the relationship is destined for disaster. Remember what I said about trying to change other people previously. Relationship problems, money problems, and legal issues will be just around the corner.

- If you are family oriented and like to spend some time at home and your mate does not like or want children and like to party 24/7, there will be issues. Especially if you want kids, and your partner does not, this will put a strain on the relationship. Also, if you and your mate disagree about how to raise your kids once, you have them there will be problems; especially if you do so in front of your kids, there will always be arguments. Issues regarding children are one of the major causes of arguments and breakups in relationships especially blended situations.

- If your mate feels like their only family is the one that they were born into and you do not, it is not going to be long before you start feeling like a third wheel. In this type of relationship, the mate's family usually does not respect you and the disrespect from the mate will soon follow in some form. Especially if your mate needs his family or friend's approval on everything, he or she does and everyone he or she is dating. Real men and women make their own decisions. If they cannot, there will always be trouble in your relationship.

- If you and your mate were born in different periods, you might find it difficult to relate to each other. The greater the distance between your ages the more likely you will not be able to relate to each other. I am not saying it cannot work; I am saying that it will be a challenge. I have seen it repeatedly.

- If your mate feels and acts as if real communication is a form of nagging and you do not, there will be some difficult days ahead. Especially if they feel this way when they have disrespected you or your relationship. There is a difference between nagging and communicating, and we all know the difference. Too often people who are being deceitful in a relationship use this as an excuse. If they are really into you, they will want to communicate. I do not care what someone has told you about men and communicating. Real men communicate.

- If you want one thing out of the relationship and your mate wants another it will never work. For example, you want love, fidelity, and commitment and they want a place to stay or be until they find "the one". Let us just face it. If this is your situation, you will probably not ever be 'the one". Let us say you have been dating this person for a while, and you would like them to take to the next level but they do not. If you manage to coerce them down the aisle, it probably will not last unless you plan to ignore and cope with the situation the rest of your life. You should not waste your valuable time. You do not want to wake up ten years down the road in the same "wait and see" or promise ring state. When people wish to take a relationship to the next level, they will not need prompting or coercing.

- If you enjoy romance and sex and your mate does not, there will always be problems. I believe preceded by a lack of communication and money and followed by issues surrounding children, sex *(too little or too much)* is another major cause of arguments and break up in relationships. One must remember that if they attracted someone with the spice of "dropping it like it's hot," twirling on poles or jumping from the ceilings they will have to keep it up. I am only kidding about jumping from the ceiling; however, you get the point.

- If you are self-reliant, and your mate is a parasite, it will never work. Come on now, you know what a parasite does. It is someone that lives off the energy and efforts of others without giving anything useful in return. Unless you have made it a habit picking up the phone and dialing an escort service or picking up prostitutes off the street, sex should not be the only thing you are getting in return. This person does not constitute a mate. If you would like to rid yourself of a parasite, just stop giving so freely of your resources. You do not have to worry; they will be off to the next host shortly. Either they will leave you, or they will make it so unbearable for you to live with them until you leave. This way they do not feel as guilty. It does not matter either way you will be free and freedom, in this case, is a good thing.

- If your mate feels that it is O.K. to have another or others on the side, and you do not, it will not be long before trouble comes knocking at your door. If you get or stay involved, you will need to be able to deal with the drama that this type of relationship will bring. Trust me. There will be drama, and it will be just around the corner. I am always puzzled at the analysis some people and experts say regarding cheating. Does it matter why some people cheat? The fact that they do should be enough. Some people feel that it has something to do with them or the other person. They feel they were not pretty enough, rich enough, smart enough, etc. However, many times it has nothing to do with them at all, it is just who the cheater is as a person.

Experts will say that when men cheat it is not the same as women, and it is not emotional. However, this is not always the case. They forget the other person has usually cheated with someone else who is emotional and wants you to know, your family and friends to know, their family and friends to know, and the world to know they have been with your man or woman. Many of these affairs produce children. You do not think it was an accident on the other person's part do you? You can count on there being drama. It is just a matter of time. Stop settling. If you are looking for "typical" then maybe you have found the right person for "you", but if you are looking for "exceptional," keep looking. People will treat you the way you allow them to treat you. If you allow people to intimidate, manipulate, and dominate you, they are not likely to respect you. You should not allow anyone to mistreat you in any relationship. You just need to walk away and in some cases run. Run very fast. It is easy to stay; however, it takes courage to walk away. You have that courage within you. You just need to find it sooner than later.

As a woman, we all have probably heard the saying "Men will be men." Some cultures practice this idea. Once upon a time humankind was naked and ran around in the bush. In a primitive culture or world, this concept might reign supreme; however, since civilization and the advancement of people you cannot tell me that a real man or a real woman is incapable of not running around in the streets and humping everything in sight. That would be the equivalent of a dog. An excuse that some use to justify what they are doing or what someone is doing to them. Remember that the subject of this book is about finding, enjoying and keeping real love. The key word is "real". Real love is like real gold. There is a difference between real gold and fool's gold. Fool's gold only resembles real gold and is not valuable at all. After saying all this, if you encounter fool's love, just keep it moving forward. It should not be the right situation for you unless that is what you want. However, you shouldn't complain later when it all falls apart. Trust me it will break down, or you will become the best at coping in some way.

The right mate simply should be a part of your dream team. It will help you further your other goals in life as well. People tend to be more successful in their business life when their personal life is on track. Finding the right balance is essential. You will spend less time and energy trying to clean up all the nightmares from having the wrong person in your life. You will have someone to grow in love with rather than grow apart. You win or lose by what you choose, and you always win big by choosing right the first time.

There is someone for everyone. You cannot beat yourself up or feel guilty for making the best choices in life for yourself. It is your life. I know people will put all types of demands on you and tell you that you are judgmental; however, it is not judgmental to want to choose the best situation for yourself. There is someone right for them with the same type of situations. It just should not be you. Common sense should tell us oil and water do not mix. Why would you try to mix two entirely different lifestyles together and expect them to blend into one well?

Before you begin to maintain, you need to ask yourself three questions:

(1) Am I up to code?

(2) Is my significant other up to code?

(3) Is the situation up to code?

# Chapter Three

# Enjoy and Keep Real Love by Maintaining

Like a house, every relationship needs maintenance for upkeep, or it will fall apart over time if left unattended. Have you ever wondered why people need a building permit to construct a house? It is required to protect the consumer from shady contractors who perform below standard work. If the structure is not up to code, it will not pass inspection and will be dangerous to its inhabitants. Before we begin to maintain, we need to ask ourselves three questions: Am I up to code, is my significant other up to code, and is the situation up to code? If you have the right building materials and the construction is up to code, maintenance will be an easier task. The next three sections deal with maintaining your "House of Love". Let us now look at the last three ingredients within those sections that you will need in your "House of Love" for maintenance: Have the acronym TRUST, Put in the Work and Pay Attention to the Signs.

The acronym *TRUST* must be in a relationship for it to work:

**T**alk
**R**espect
**U**nderstanding
**S**haring
**T**olerance

## 3:1　Have the Acronym TRUST

After you have chosen the right mate, you and your mate must both be trustworthy and have faith that your relationship will work. You must be able to rely on each other. You will need to be able to have faith. You both must rely on the fact that the other will be there for you, have your back, do what is right for the two of your relationship, communicate with you, respect you, understand, share their life with you, have tolerance for those things that are important to you and love you. You must earn trust; therefore, if you have not earned trust, you should not expect it. I always use the acronym TRUST to help explain what it means to me. The meaning of my acronym is as follows:


**T**alk
**R**espect
**U**nderstanding
**S**haring
**T**olerance


I have chosen the above as the acronym because they all have elements of trust within them. What I like about each one is that they each have elements of the others within them. Let us look at each one further:

**Talk.** Here I am referring to communication when talking about "Talk". You must have good communication for your relationship to work. Talk and listen to each other. Communication involves talking, listening, understanding, sharing, tolerance and respect. Lack of proper or appropriate communication is another leading cause of breakups in a relationship. People communicate with those they trust. However, if they fear undue criticism from their mate, they will not. Communicate with your significant other in a way that enhances your relationship instead of destroying it. Communication should occur without unconstructive criticism. People like to hear that you love and appreciate them more than they want to hear what you think about their faults. Especially if you only wish to communicate with them when you feel a need to point out your partner's faults. The goal should be to build and uplift not tear down regularly. Avoid being a constant "dream snatcher" or "ego buster". If the person is so horrible that you cannot appreciate them, they do not need talking with, they need running from, and you have again chosen the wrong mate.

Relationships should not be a guessing game. How will they know your likes and dislikes, your dreams and desires, what turns you on or off or what is going on with the finances if you do not tell them? If they know what you like, chances are you will receive it on a regular basis. A major part of communicating is listening to both verbal and non-verbal cues. You will never be able to understand if you do not listen. Good communication adds to the success of your relationship. If you have trouble communicating, you will always have trouble relating.

I know you probably heard the advice that men dread the words "we need to talk"; however, like most problems in a relationship, this is only an issue if you have chosen the wrong mate. Seems always to come back to the concept of choosing the right partner again. I cannot stress how important this key ingredient will be for a healthy relationship. The right person will care about you, what you think, and your feelings. They will want to listen and talk.

Communication should not occur with anger. You do not have to shout to communicate. If you have gotten to know the other person, you will know which buttons to push to make the other angry. Unless anger is your intent, you should avoid pushing those buttons. I had someone tell me once that every time he got ready to see someone else on a particular night or weekend, he would start a verbal fight with his mate and his mate would ask him to leave. While the other person thought they were just cooling off, they would be free to see other people. They said they could always go back and makeup. If this is always happening to you, maybe you should reevaluate your relationship. Remember "The Golden Rule" we all learned in kindergarten. It applies here as well. You should always speak to people the way you want them to talk to you.

Conflicts will happen in your relationship, but they do not need to get out of hand. Here are a few tips for communicating during conflicts that will make fighting fair:

> **Speak kind words and be aware of your body language and actions.** No name-calling, shouting, screaming, bullying *(throwing things or intimidating)*, or intentionally bringing up known weaknesses or sensitive issues (known as "hitting below the belt"). No rolling of the eyes, throwing up the hand in the other person's face *(as in "talk to the hand")* or laying on of the hands *(as in hitting)*.

> **Listen.** Do not walk away while your partner is trying to communicate. Do not intentionally cut your partner off while they are communicating. You will need to listen actively. One way to actively listen is to restate back to your partner what you understood them to say. Communication is always a two-way street. Sometimes you will learn it was all a misunderstanding.

> **Find a common ground.** Usually, in most conflicts and arguments there is a common ground you will both share. This common ground is a good starting point.

> **Use "I" instead of "You"** when stating your feelings to avoid your partner being very defensive or counterattacking you. When you use the word "You", it accuses and blames the other person. No one wants to feel like the bad guy even if they are. For example, say, "I understood what was said to be XYZ and that made me feel sad."

> **Focus on the present as opposed to past grievances.** Don't dwell in the past unless you are trying to show a pattern of behavior that has continued. Sometimes people's past is their present and future. They just have not gotten it yet and have no plans of modifying their behavior.

> **Avoid saving up hurts and hostilities** as future weapons and then dump then on your partner all at once. Do you remember the saying some of our parents would tell us when we were younger? I am going to get you for "old and new". Well, we all

are not kids anymore and just like when we were kids we will not remember what you are punishing us for or even what our mate is talking about if they do not deal with the problem at the appropriate time.

➢ **Avoid pushing each other's buttons.** If you have gotten to know your partner as you should have done, you know what to say that will make them mad. *(Always think before you speak.)*.

➢ **Admit it when you are wrong and apologize.**

➢ **Don't skip around the "mulberry bush".** Communication should not be a guessing game. With some people, you must get straight to the point. Say what you mean and mean what you say.

➢ **Avoid going to bed angry.** Not going to bed angry and waking up angry is a concept my husband introduced to our relationship and I agreed from the beginning. It forces you to communicate and work things out. No matter how big or small the disagreement, we always communicate and work it out before our heads hit the pillow. After twenty-one years of marriage, we have never been separated once not even overnight angry at each other.

**Respect.** You and your mate should have respect for yourselves, each other, your children, and your parents. If you have respect in these areas, your relationship will have a good chance of survival. People usually have respect for those that they trust.

You must first have respect for yourself. This advice especially holds true for the young ladies. My grandmother and momma would always say, "Child, if they can get the milk free, there will be no need to purchase the cow." My grandma and momma had a lot of good common sense. If you do not respect yourself, the other person is not likely to have respect for you either. You should seek to have a vertical relationship first before you have a horizontal one. Sometimes horizontal relationships never turn into vertical ones. We all know of someone who was in a lengthy bad relationship through years of living together, sometimes multiple kids and the other person met someone else, picked up immediately and married them sometimes in less than a year. Now the one remaining is broken hearted and left trying to raise children by themselves while usually attempting to run the other person down for support. In this type of relationship, the person was never "the one", just "the one right now". It is never in your best interest to play house. The odds will not be in your favor.

Having respect for each other is crucial. You should respect each other to put the other first before others in your relationship. Respect each other, share, and speak kind words to one another. Respect each other enough to keep others out of your business. It will be essential to maintaining your "House of Love". To keep real love, you must first keep others out of your business.

Finally, you must have and show respect to each other's parents. If it were not for them, your mate would not be here. Even if your in-laws or soon to be in-laws are from some place down under, you should not remind your partner every chance you get. It is always better to communicate to your partner your feelings when you feel someone is mistreating you. If you are the one, he or she will address issues when and if it arises.

In summation, you should always follow "The Golden Rule" and provide mutual respect by treating your partner and others the way you would want them to treat you. Always treat the other with respect. If it is someone, you cannot respect, they are not the person for you, and you should not waste your valuable time.

**Understanding.** You and your mate must have an understanding of the way the other feels. As mentioned earlier, you must communicate which involves talking, listening, understanding, and sharing. If you listen to them, the other will trust you enough to convey the valuable information you will need to understand them. We know this as sharing. If you understand each other, you both will be able to have tolerance and avoid those trivial things that push each other's buttons and starts unnecessary arguments. You both must also understand that if your relationship does not have the essential ingredients mentioned in this guide, it is not likely to have staying power and be healthy.

**Sharing.** You must share your lives with each other. If they trust you, they will be willing to share their world with you. It is important for the both of you to share things with one another for mutual benefit. Share your ideas, dreams and hopes. Sharing is part of communicating which involves talking. Share laughter, fun, excitement, struggles and responsibility. Take turns doing something the other likes to do. You just might discover something new that you will enjoy as well. If you are married, do not forget the small stuff that is usually not small regarding importance. You must share the responsibilities *(chores, picking up the kids if you have children, and etc.)*. You should worship together. If you have chosen the right mate, this will be easy to do. There is nothing that I hate to see worse than couples who live separate lives. If you did not just know they were together, you would not have a clue that they were a couple. They are just passing through the years in apathy. If you are with someone who is not willing to share, he or she may have secrets that prevent him or her from sharing. If sharing is an issue, they are not the right mate. You will not have to beg the "right man or woman for you" to share. They will not leave you staring at the four walls by yourself every Friday or Saturday night and holidays. You will not have the run the right mate down in the middle of the day or night. The "right" partner for you will want to share their life with you without complaining.

You must learn to share your knowledge with your sons and daughters, nieces and nephews, especially your daughters and nieces. I call this my POW2 Factor: Bridging the gap between generations between unhealthy and healthy relationships by building **P**eople of **W**isdom and **W**ealth. Knowledge is always power. You must equip them with the ability to be and stay healthy and to share love. Part of this "planting the seed" will never be in anything you will ever say. It will be in what they see you do and your relationships that they see. Part of what is wrong with the health of couples' relationships today is that one or both of the partners had no healthy role models of a relationship when they grew up, and they are just simply doing what they have seen and know. This hit home with me one day when a child approached me and said he has never seen anyone like my husband and me. It was after we finished playing a game of UNO with our child on a Friday night. It was not just the UNO game. Looking back on all he was a witness to since he had known us, he said most people do not live as we do. He said in his world, these types of things never existed and that our son is a very lucky kid. Most of my son's friends tell him and us this all the time. My heart is sad for some of their situations. Our house has become the hangout spot for the neighboring kids. We have even received phone calls to come to the emergency room for neighboring children as their parents just are not there for them. Most show up at family holiday gatherings. We don't mind because these children need someone positive in their lives. We as people have become too liberated as a culture that "whatever" has replaced morality and good common sense. While some of us are busy being selfish and having "big fun," we forget about the consequences and the children that are involved. When the children go astray, we never look at ourselves as the blame but want to talk about how "bad" they have become. They "know better" is all I hear many times. How do they know better? What have we shown them through your actions?

**Tolerance**. You must have tolerance. You both must be willing to recognize and respect the beliefs of the other. Keep in mind that if you are "equally yoked"; you will have less to tolerate. Tolerance does not mean putting up with crap that you should not have to endure. You should learn to recognize "BS" when you see and hear it. Relationships are about the right balance of giving and take from both parties. If your mate trusts you, they will be more likely to tolerate what is important to you.

If your significant other will not talk to you, does not respect you, does not understand you, will not share with you, and has no tolerance, how can you ever trust him or her and why are they still your mate? They are not trustworthy, and you need to return to the keys "Get to Know the Other Person and Choose the Right Mate for You" in the previous sections.

The *"Love"* in *"I Love You"* is an action verb.

If there are no actions that reflects / resemble love after someone has said it to you, it should mean nothing to you.

## 3:2   Put in the Work

Now that you have all the previous keys and have the right materials, it is time to put in the work. "Happily Ever After" will be within your reach if you are willing to put in the work. The "Love" in "I Love You" is an action verb.   If there are no actions that reflect/resemble love after someone has said it to you, it should mean nothing to you.   Taking action is the only way we can turn our dreams into realities; otherwise, they are just wishes.   In a relationship, this does not mean actions from only one person.   You must both be willing to do the work.

### Where to Start?

The type of work that you will put in will depend on you and your mate.  If you have gotten to know one another, this will not be difficult. Putting in the work is where you need to bring that "good, good" and plenty of it.  The "good, good" is whatever you and your mate like that fulfill your desires and makes you happy.  I am not just talking about sex here although it is a part of it.  Putting in the work also means fulfilling your responsibilities and the TRUST elements talked about previously as well as romance and intimacy.

Marriage and love can be fun if you have all the right essential ingredients and make it that way by putting in the work.  Where do you start?  Firstly, it goes without saying that you both need to handle your business outside of and between the sheets.  Here's a dose of wisdom for you.  It's very wise people that understand their significant other's psychological needs and meets them.   Very wise people share the responsibility of finances and children in their home.  Very wise people handle their business between the sheets, and that should not be exclusive to just between the sheets.

Here are a few other suggestions on where to start: If you are about to get married, you should begin by making your honeymoon memorable.  If you are married, you should start by making your anniversaries memorable. You may think that there is no need for me to mention this; however, you would be surprised at the people that go to bed as if it is any other day. Don't forget birthdays, Mother's Day and Father's Day, Christmas if you are a Christian and Valentine's Day. In addition to Valentine's Day, send flowers and candy or whatever your mate like just because it is Monday, Tuesday, Wednesday, Thursday, Friday, Saturday or Sunday. The day does not matter. It is the thought that counts and you need to make your "thoughts" count. You need to stroke each other's ego. I will not mention how as that is different for different people. Take day trips, night trips or weekend getaways. If your mate's car is dirty, wash it or have it detailed. Can we all please learn how to prepare and cook a meal or, at least, a dish? To me, there is nothing sexier than when you have finished handling your business in the bedroom that your man or woman gets up the next morning and prepares you your favorite breakfast in bed and says I just wanted you to know how much I enjoyed last night and this morning. It is part of the after play, and it work well for foreplay as well. There is nothing more mood breaking to me than having to wait until your husband or wife wakes up, and then you two have to put on some clothes and try and find something to eat. Everything you need should be right there or a phone call away to be delivered. How about a marathon of just spending an entire rainy day in bed? Trust me, if you are with the right person, they will enjoy doing this one. If you have kids, you can be creative and prearrange for the children to spend the weekend with their grandparents. I sometimes hear people make a lot of excuses. There should not be consistent excuses.

Imagine when someone respects and puts you first in your relationship this is a part of putting in the work. This is an action of love. Imagine them only having $20 in their wallet and sharing it with you so that you can have lunch to eat. Don't confuse this with only having $20 in the bank. That is another conversation. Imagine you waking up in the morning and entering the bathroom and your significant other has written the words "I Love You" on the mirror from the condensation from the shower just because they want to brighten your morning. Imagine opening your lunch bag and finding an uplifting note that makes your day. Imagine coming home from a long, hard day of work and dinner is already on the table or they tell you they are taking you out to eat tonight. Imagine going to the gas station on a cold winter's day and your mate shows up to pump you gas so that you do not have to get out of the car in the cold. Maybe they show up at the grocery store to help you put the groceries in the car, and you did not ask them too. I am not talking about stalking. Imagine meeting an acquaintance of your mate who he just introduced you to and the acquaintance says that he is glad, he finally met you because his friend must love you as you are all he talks about all the time. Certainly different from hearing, "Oh, I didn't know you two were together" or "Who is this"? By now, you get the picture.

Sometimes it is just looking at your mate and smiling and when they ask you why you are smiling say, "I still find you as beautiful as the day we met." You should tell them what makes them beautiful to you. It is awesome when you and your mate can say "I STILL" after so many years. This list is endless; however, the key is to know your partner and to know what he or she will appreciate and make sure they receive plenty of it on a regular basis. It is the "Good and Plenty".

Another place to start is to make yourself feel good first. When you feel good, you can make someone else feel good also. For example, I do not know about you, but I love spa days. When I get my hair done, get my nails and toes done, get a body massage or have a bubble bath, and I have on "pretty panties," I feel sexy. For me, there is power in "pretty panties". The power of the "pretty panties" concept is another book. I have included this idea in some of the workshops that I have conducted, and the participants have enjoyed it. Yes, I have even included it in a workshop I did at a women's conference at a church. All I am trying to say is that when you make yourself feel good, it will go a long way in your relationship. If you want to see your mate in pretty panties or underwear and want to introduce them to more colors in the crayon box of underwear other than white, you simply need to buy them and stop waiting for them to get a hint.

It goes without saying, the work you put in should be your work and not someone else's. Here is a prime example. Someone often criticizes me that my husband and I do not have any fun. However, that is the furthest thing from the truth. We just do not advertise everything we do to the masses. He or she says that I am always shut up in the house, and we should not make everything about my son. On a whim, we will go out of town to a neighboring state to one of our favorite restaurants &, etc. After we have made safe provision for our son, we do get to have some private time alone to enjoy ourselves. We just do not go partying every weekend. Our son is the priority now, and we have afforded him with all the opportunities in life a child should have that we could afford to help him grow into a stable, self-sufficient adult. It is what my parents provided for me and why wouldn't I not want my son to have as good as or better than I had in life. Once he is old enough to be on his own, we then can become the priority. My husband and I do not feel the time we spent volunteering as a Cub Scout leader and going to countless sporting events was a burden. It was enjoyable. The time I spend "shut up in my house," I was working on my projects while my husband and son were off on day hunting trips. "On your terms" should be your new phrase for the century. You should enjoy life on your terms, not someone else's terms. Too many of our children are left neglected to fend for themselves. If my kid goes astray in his adult life, it will not be because he was not taught and shown better. He is growing up in a home filled with love. He has never seen or heard us physically fighting. We have had disagreements as all couples do and he has seen us work them out like adults should. To date, my husband and I have never left each other, and you better believe, we both put in the work.

Putting in work with the wrong person is a waste of time. I have always been on point with mine. Therefore, if a relationship that I was in did not work, I knew it couldn't have been me. There is not an ex that I have ever had that can say I was lacking in anything. However, I must say that if you are putting in the work and it is one sided, you have chosen the wrong mate. Why would they be worth your time when you obviously are not worth their time. Here is my example. I was once in a relationship and I was passing the GYM where my significant other worked out and I saw his car there. Because I was extremely busy with a full time job, college full time and modeling with this agency, I got the idea that I would leave him a note to let him know that although my schedule was very busy, I was thinking of him. It was a poem I had written. I left the note and continued on my way. The man told me that was one of the craziest things he had ever seen. He actually said, "Who does that? That is crazy!" He then started referring to me as weird. It broke my spirit. Because of his continued actions, eventually we broke up. Later, he came back to me and said he just wanted me to know there was never anything wrong with me. He told me the following: *"I did certain things to try to keep you in check. I was seeing other women and I really couldn't have you just popping up places if you saw my car. When I was in the chase and we had a date I would purposely start an argument with you so that I would be free to go about my business. I also knew you had love for me and it would not be difficult getting you to forgive me. As for the other women, they never had anything over you. They were spending their money on me and you were spending what little money you had on college and your younger siblings. You still live at home with your parents and some of them had apartments. It may have been wrong of me but I initially thought I could have more with them as your parents were common people who lived a meager life.* He asked me if I could forgive him. I did forgive him but I did not take him back. I finally learned to love myself more. Forgiveness and reconciliation are two different things. It was a perfect situation for his lifestyle. I lived out of town, I was extremely busy, I was nice and a lot of fun. I feel the work I put in this relationship was wasted. I always wanted to be able to take care of myself so no person would ever hold me in bondage. Yes, he was correct, I was not spending money on him if it was not his birthday, Valentine's day or Christmas. The truth is that my cousin told me that she met some women at work that told her that this man and his friend used women for what they could get out of them in terms of money and other material things. She said she told them that she knew for a fact that he was not using her cousin. She was correct. He presented himself to me to be as sweet and kind as I was kind. He never once asked me for money or any material things. In the beginning, we could talk about anything. He would always tell me "you are a good girl and I like that and you love me and I you". In the beginning, he was the perfect man. He was just as sweet to me as I was to him. That is how I fell for him. We never argued about anything, but in the end when I finally stopped for a second, got up and looked to see why this man had started to disrespect me emotionally I did not like what I found. During this time, other men approached me in college that were good candidates as far as a boyfriend goes but I was trying to be true to something that was not true to me. Some of them were beautiful people *(inside and out)* from great families who would go on to have amazing careers. I did not know the truth about my situation and to get with one of those other guys would have been cheating. I had first saw him when I was a teenager. We started dating when I was about 17 or 18.

I still stayed at home and worked so I could afford things that were important to me *(a college education, traveling, helping my family, and other woman stuff)*. When I could afford it, I would take my younger sister who was still in school to the salon. It was something that I never had the opportunity to experience when I was younger and I wanted to show her what it was like to receive special treatment. Money at that time was tight for me and once I had to choose whether to get her hair done or mine and I chose to get hers done. I have always had a good heart. In the end I had discovered a lot of things that were not true when it came to him. The lies hurt me greatly. You should put in the work in an environment that is conducive to something positive with someone that is right for you. When I woke up and started putting in the work in the right place, my God blessed immensely in my life and I am so grateful.

## Making Love and Enjoying Sex

Now let us speak of "Making Love and Enjoying Sex." Hopefully, you have chosen and married the right mate and you both actual enjoy making love and having sex. Making love and having sex are two different things. You will need to bring the right mix of both. There is nothing more frustrating in a relationship than when men and women do not handle their business and leave their mates hanging left to either please themselves or worse they sin and seek pleasure from somewhere else. If you view it as a duty, then that is what it will feel like to your mate. If it has come to that, then something has broken down in the communication and spice process, and you two need to have a conversation as to why you don't enjoy it and it feels like "a chore or duty" and see if you can fix it. I will have to say to both sexes that you can't be slacking in other areas of your relationship and expect the sheets to be any better. If you tear each other down on a regular basis rather than uplifting each other, you can expect "the sheets" to be torn down as well.

Your mate is more likely to desire you physically if you make them feel good about their self; they feel loved by you, close to you, supported by you and protected by you. I just have one curious question to ask.

What kind of mate do some of you have where they have time and energy to have extra people on the side? If you are holding it down like you should be in all other aspects and handling your business in the bedroom, you will not have time for anything else. You will probably need to get some rest/sleep and allow the soreness to reside from some sessions unless your mate requires very little in that department; however, these should have been questions to explore before you jumped. Don't get me wrong I am not saying that sex should be rough. It should be very enjoyable and fun. What I am saying is in exploration and depending on duration and frequency; especially if you have high stamina, sometimes sensitive areas do become a little sore, but it's that "good and plenty" kind of sore. Well, enough of that, you should get the picture about what your responsibility is to your mate in this area. Learn what they like, tell or show them what you like and just deliver it on a regular.

Earlier I mentioned, "enough spice to fuel the fire." It is my opinion that sex is a physiological *(basic)* need. Some people feel after they get married and when they find religion, they are supposed to forget about their selves and their spouse. Making love and having sex in a marriage is another part of putting in the work; however, it should be enjoyable. Spice is different for different people. Communication comes into play in this situation. It is the only way you will find out which spices your mate prefers over the others. You both must tell the other what turns you on. Once you find out, make sure you deliver it on a regular. That is the "plenty". Be sure to introduce new things *(positions, places, &)* occasionally. Most of all it should be enjoyable for both parties as stated earlier. If it is the right man or woman, they will want to experience new things with you. Remember this was one of the questions on the "Before You Jump List." So hopefully, you chose someone who feels the same about love making and sex as you do.

*Real love cannot be found where it does not exist; therefore, there should be some reflections of love.*

## 3:3　Pay Attention to the Signs

How will you know if someone loves you? You will know it by their actions. The "Know" is always in the "Show". Don't confuse this with some people's twisted versions of what "I Love You" means. Sometimes when people say, "I Love You" what they mean is:

- "I like you."
- "I am attracted to you." *(Lust and Love are two different things.)*
- "I want or need something from you, and you like to hear it."
- "I just got caught doing something, and I need you to believe me."
- "I like the things you buy for me."
- "I love the things you do to me sexually."
- "This situation is convenient for me and if you leave who is going to help pay these bills."

The above are some of the real reasons why actions do not resemble love in some relationships. People will sometimes lie, but consistent actions rarely do. Signs of real actions of love must exist. We sometimes get in the habit of making excuses for people when "real love" was never there. If your partner gives you a dozen yellow roses on Valentine day and your favorite color is not yellow, the chances are that it is not love.

If the actions of love are there, you will know it. If not, stop waiting for them to appear month after month and year after year in the wrong person. Just face it. They are not into you, and they should not be "the one" for you. You cannot find real love where it does not exist. You see real women *(unless they don't require much)* like real men. Men who say what they mean and mean what they say and their actions reflect it; otherwise, they are fake wannabees and a waste of time. They say they are or want to be your man or woman in an exclusive relationship but act like you are their "jump off." A "jump off" is someone used basically for sex. Let's just face it, either you are someone's significant other or you are their "jump off" unless you and your significant other or wife role play and that is just one of your many roles; however, that's another chapter or book. People stop being someone's jump off unless that is what you want to be; however, you need to be honest about it up front. For example, if you are a man or a woman and all you want is sex then say it and mean it. While the person you are chasing may not be the one for you, just keep it moving as there is someone out there who is right for you and want the same things as you. Always remember to be safe and use protection. The wages of sex outside of marriage are usually high and you must realize when you play grown-up games *(having sex)* grown up things can and often happen, and you must be prepared to deal with the consequences if and when they do.

## A Rose is a Rose is a Rose or Is It?

Growing up my mother introduced me to flowers at an early age. My mom would make me work in her flower garden, watering and pulling out the weeds so that the flowers could stay healthy, thrive and grow. I hated this chore at the time. However, over the years the lessons, I learned in the process of taken care of her flowers taught me some valuable lessons about growth and life. I love flowers now; they are truly beautiful, and I use them often in my comparisons about love, life, and courage. Let look at some common meaning of the color of roses I have learned over the years:

| <u>**Color**</u> | <u>**Common Meaning**</u> |
|---|---|
| Red | Love |
| Yellow | Friendship |
| Mix of Red & Yellow | Unity |
| White | Pure or innocence |
| Pink | Appreciation |

If you have lived in the world, you should know that the universal symbol of love is a red rose. The next time you want to give someone a rose refer to the chart to get the meaning you want to convey correct.

## Do Not Mislead

You should never lead anyone on. That is wrong. You should never do the following when you do not love:

- Tell someone you love them when you do not
- Expect them to do things inappropriate for a friendship *(i.e. have sex with you and be exclusive to you)*
- Give them red roses
- Except or give expensive gifts
- Go out with them repeatedly
- Treat your jump off as the girlfriend else they may start thinking they are a girlfriend and have the same rights as one
- See your jump off outside the hours of midnight – 6:00 a.m.
- Take photos or videos
- Never bring them to your home or relative homes
- Give them your house number or primary cell number
- Take them to family events or events held by close friends

The next time Valentines rolls around, and you want to give someone roses, and you do not love them or barely know them then the color of the rose should not be red. Better yet, give candy instead. If you receive phone calls at night, way, way after dark to ask you if they can come over or for you to come over when it is time to go to bed, that is not love. It is a b_ _ty call. The same applies around lunchtime and 5 o'clock when people usually get off from work and want make a quick stop before they go home. It is hard for someone to love someone he or she does not respect. If you are going to fornicate and I am not suggesting you should *(just trying to keep it real)*, do not be willing to give up "the milk and cookies" to quickly. Make them have to earn them. I do agree with another now-famous author's 90day rule or, at least, it need to be a two (2) months or a 60day rule. Did not your parents or grandparents always tell you "you will appreciate it more if you earn it"? The same concept should apply here. They will appreciate it more if they have to work for it or earn it. I received a marriage proposal from my husband before we involved love making or sex in our relationship, and we were in our thirties. My husband said he could get "just sex" from anywhere, but he had been around the world and was looking for something more than "just sex." He wanted someone he could spend the rest of his life with, and he saw that someone in me. Talk about romantic to me. That still today blows my mind when I think about it. When I asked him later how did he know the love making and sex would be good, he told me he could tell and even though he was extremely attracted to me, he wanted to see if there was more. He had prayed and asked God to send him someone he could spend the rest of his life with, and then he met me, someone, he felt was not a pretender and had a pure heart just like his heart. He did not live in the state as I did and his work took him all over the world. He asked me if he could write and call me. It was incredible how much we had in common, and the communication was great. I wrote him poems during this time. He kept them, and I have them still this very day. The love poems I wrote him, I included in my book, "Love, Life, and Courage *(Poetry for the Soul)*." When his travels slowed down, he told me he had made up his mind that I was the person he wanted to spend the rest of his life with and was offering me his love forever until death do us part. He told me we had become friends but wanted to know if I would consider being his wife, his lover, the mother of his babies and his everything forever. He said that his experiences had been many but I was the most beautiful person he has ever met in his life by far, and he was not just talking about looks. I am here to tell you that there is someone out there for you, but you just need to stop looking in all the wrong places and focus on making you the best you, you can be so that your light will shine bright just like mines did. Trust me, love will find you. If it found me, it can find you.

You should not mislead people. Many times when people say that others are a pest and will not leave them alone what has happened is that they have been leading someone to believe that they are in a relationship with them. If they are not "the one", "the girl" as opposed to "that girl", or your significant other, you need to stop treating them like you are in a real relationship. Don't misled them to think they are "the one" by giving them red roses, taking them to family functions repeatedly, having them around your kids, and telling them that you love them just to get something that you want from them. The meaning of this is called "using." It gets confusing. They too are looking for "the one". All I am saying is everyone needs to be on the same page. People need to stop misleading people then turning around and trashing them by saying they are too needy or possessive. In a real relationship, individuals who love each other want to spend time with each other, want to communicate, are healthily jealous, and want to build a life together. People also need to stop being a coward and tweeting their single and available status when you know you have messed up and misled someone to believe that they are in a relationship with them without telling them first.

## The Levels of Intercourse Between Men & Women

You must be aware of the levels of intercourse between some men and women. Intercourse occurs in love, sex, and "hitting it". While making love and sex do occur in relationships and contain emotions, do not confuse "only sex without emotions" or "hitting it" with dating or being someone's girlfriend. It is merely "scratching an itch" and it require no emotions. Unless all you want is sex, it is a waste of your time and a risky practice. Occasionally but very rarely do "hitting it" progress into love. It progresses into some deep, intense lust maybe. I once heard a woman who thought she was in a relationship tell a man, "I love you". I listened to that same man say to her, "baby, I love to _____ and your _____ is good". Unfortunately, she still did not get it. I guess she thought she could change him. He never changed for this woman. He married a woman that was not giving it up to him that he respected and loved. He is not the same person he was when he was in the streets. From talking with some guys and some women over the years, I discovered a problem. The problem is that most of the women I spoke to are looking for all the things on their list in one person while a few of the males, on the other hand, were looking for different things in different women, especially when it came to "hitting it." Therefore, those men do not necessarily consider someone they are just having sex with without emotions or just "hitting it" with as someone they are dating. They are simply just having sex while the women think she is a relationship. I know you know of men who have a girlfriend or wife that they hold high on a pedestal but have jump offs that they have to do everything under the sun. For some, it was not that their wife will not do certain things. It was that some men said they do not want their wife or girlfriend to do certain things. They felt certain things to them were considered whoring, and they did not wish to think of their significant other like a whore. Also, there was this one woman I overheard talking telling her girlfriend that the male in her life was only providing sex for money. She said that she did not want to get married to him as he was someone else husband. She preferred it to stay that way because when he finished, she could send him back home for someone else to wash his "dirty ____". Seemed strange coming from a woman, but that is what I overheard. I hate to put it harshly but it is what it is and to some people that are all that it is. That's all I am saying. Ladies, I do have to tell you that if he is only "hitting it" in the car, in the bathroom at the club or work, in the closet or parking lot, you are not dating, and he is not your man. Also, if he is only seeing you in the late hours of the night or early hours of the morning for sex and you are not already in a relationship with him, and you all are not having a role playing session, you are not dating, and he is not your man. A lot of times men will not come out and say; I'm just want to have sex or "hit it"; especially if they feel you will not have intercourse with them otherwise. You have seen the news reports; especially from famous people. He is usually rumored to be with or photographed with different women who reporters say are his girlfriends only for him to tweet or say his status is single and available. Unless you want to be "that girl", keep it moving. These types of buddies rarely end up as anything more except for someone "baby daddy or baby momma". If this is your goal, then I guess you are on the right track for that. As said earlier, having sex eventually leads to consequences. If you want to be someone's "baby momma" get them to put a ring on it first and say those vows. Based on what I learned from working with children over the years and the friends I grew up with, your future child will appreciate you if you take this route.

## When in Doubt, Check It Out

You deserve to be informed and sometimes your life depends on it. You must remember that it is your life, and you should not be afraid to ask questions. You cannot just ask people who love him or her. Although some might tell the truth, most will be biased. The reality might be that they are a dysfunctional person or family, but as far as they know, they are a nice and normal person or family. Dysfunctional people usually do not understand that they are dysfunctional. There is an old saying that you should not go looking for trouble, or you will find it. I am here to tell you that you do not have to go looking for trouble. It will eventually find you. Sometimes it finds you when you least expect it. If you are in a relationship and your gut feelings and the signs tell you that there is something wrong, you need to check it out. You can choose to keep blinders on and pretend as though nothing is going on if you would like; however, you must always remember that it was your choice and not a choice someone else forced on you. We live in a time of incurable diseases and love triangles that send people to an early grave every day. My advice is to check it out so that you can make informed decisions before it checks you out. Checking it out does not mean spending your every waking moment as an I-Spy or E-Spy or showing up somewhere starting a fight. If it has come to that, is it worth a fight? You can walk away. If you must resort to those tactics, they are not the right mate, and it is not true or real love. Joy really will come in the morning if you wake up and allow it too. Most of the time we are so busy trying to hold on to something that is not right for us or not worth holding on to that we can't see joy and happiness around the corner for all the constant drama. Drama can waste your life away. Here is something that is not a newsflash. Most of the people who get married to some people have already seen the signs of an unhealthy relationship in the making and decided to ignore them regardless of the risk factors. They then want others to feel sorry for them because they have made themselves a lifelong victim *(that is if they don't get out of it)*. You cannot change a person; especially if they do not want to change. There are such things as predators looking for prey. Always choose to be a victor over being a victim.

## When Love Hurts

Love should never hurt. It should never be emotionally or physically abusive. You should pay attention to the signs that usually lead to abuse. Your partner is or may be abusive if the following are occurring in your relationship:

- **Your partner is overly jealous or possessive.** I am not speaking of the healthy form of being jealous or someone calling you possessive because you suspect your partner is having unprotected sex with someone else at the same time as you and you just want to protect yourself. You do have the right to know. People may think this is foolish; however, I know of four people who have died of AIDS because they did not pay attention to the signs and did not check it out before it was too late.

- **Your partner abuses drugs or alcohol.** It will not be long before they start abusing you and may not remember half of it. Some people do not remember the things they have done while being high. It will be easy for them to forget who you are. Growing up, I mostly had friends who were guys. When I was in my twenties, I remember one of my friend guys telling us that he needed to stop drinking so much as he ended up in some woman's bed and don't remember how it happen or if he did anything with her or not but prays he did not. He had gone to a party with a male who he did not hang out with on a regular basis, and I know to be nobody's real friend. The drug and alcohol abusers do not make good choices in mates or friends. Therefore, I know it is the truth when some people say they don't remember some things after they come down from a high. In this case, unfortunately for him, this woman he did not love ended up pregnant and the rest of the story is a nightmare.

- **Your partner has a history of bad relationships.** What would make you think at some point that they would not do the same to you either physically or emotionally? I once knew a woman that people told not to marry a particular man because his first wife was mysteriously found dead. People suspected him but could not prove it. She married him regardless of the facts. After years of abuse, he finally killed her. Had it not been for the children seeing him putting something in the truck of his car and the bicycle, which he rode back home on, he would have never been caught. The authority would have never resumed his first wife's body, and they would have never determined that he killed them by the same method. They served justice in the end; however, neither the first wife nor the second wife are here. I went to school and played softball with these women.

- **Your partner comes from a family of abusive relationships, and someone abused them as a child.** Abusive behavior will seem normal to them.

- **Your partner is constantly accusing you of cheating, flirting or having a roaming eye.**

- **Your partner isolates you from your family and friends, and your family and friends are not criminals, abusive or dysfunctional.**

- **You partner constantly belittles, humiliates, or make you feel shame in front of others.**

- **Your partner consistently blames you for their emotional shortcomings or problems.**

- **Your partner is violent or loses their temper quickly.** It usually occurs for a little of nothing. If you are always on pins and needles wondering if they will be mad, then this is occurring.

- **Your partner threatens to hurt or kill you**. They usually can and eventually will.

- **You partner pushes, shoves, slaps, kicks, hits or punch you.**
- **Your partner blames you when they hurt you**. "Look what you made me do" will become commonplace.

- **You cannot get out of a bad relationship.** Your partner quit you previously, or you left them. You will not take them back, and they will not let you go.

If your relationship has any of the above signs, you need not pursue it any further, get out and seek help. The physical abuse may not be there at first. It could be years; however, you should watch for outraged, uncontrollable anger and emotional abuse. Physical abuse is usually right around the corner behind it when the situation presents itself; especially if they perceive you to do something that ticks them off. If you or someone you know need help, you can call the National Domestic 24-Hour Toll-Free Hotline at 1-800-799-SAFE *(7233)*. They will ask you if it's safe to talk. You must speak the truth. You must remember silence is a catalyst for violence. If an abuser knows that their words and deeds will not remain hidden, it will make many of them think twice before victimizing someone again.

I am too familiar with "When Love Hurts". I was once in a relationship with someone that I thought was the "perfect man." He never once did or said anything out of the way that would cause me to think otherwise. He was always so respectful toward me, proud of me, and showed me, love. We would talk about dreams and how to make those dreams come true. I helped him start a business and in return, he was to help me pay for law school. Then, the rumors started. People tell a lot of young women they should not go looking for trouble in a relationship due to rumors, and like the ones that listen to them, I never did go looking until it was almost too late. I was too busy with my life. When I would ask him about the rumors, he would tell me that they were just haters who did not want to see us together. Then he would say to me, "don't I always treat you good? Well, you have nothing to worry about because I Love You. He started talking about getting married, and we began looking at houses. However, when the rumors started to come from reliable sources, I could not ignore them anymore. When I finally did check things out, I learned that the rumors were true. When I confronted him, and our relationship was ending, the signs of potential abuse all began to show. He expected me to understand that he lied to me because he knew I would not see him otherwise even though it ruined my reputation. He also expected me to be willing to be his No. 1 with the big house; nice car & etc. and no one or nothing else mattered if he gave me the world. When we broke up and after I met someone else three months later, he bought me a ring and asked my mother to marry me. He felt it was time for us to have a child. At least, that is what he told me. I guess he felt that I was nurturing, and somehow this would fix all the wrong he had done. However, my mind overruled my heart, and I gave him his ring back. It would have been easier to stay, but easier is not always best. I did not want to live the lifestyle filled with too many risks he was offering. In the beginning, the tears were many but with each passing day, they went away. When we broke up, he decided if he could not have me, no one else would either. He had become too attached to me. He became someone I had never known. I would never have dreamed that this man could have hurt me physically regardless of the situation. Listening to people with antiquated views almost cost me my life. Had I checked out the rumors, in the beginning, we would never have gotten so attached to each other, and things would have never gotten this far. We live in a time and age where those antique views are obsolete. You should always check the situation out before it checks you out. I only tell this in hopes that it will prevent someone from making the same mistake. A lot of women were not as lucky as I was in this situation.

## Quality versus Quantity in a Relationship

Your goal when starting a serious relationship should always be one of quality that will have longevity as opposed to just having longevity. The quality will allow you to weather the storms that will occur. We all are aware of relationships that have lasted for years yet are unhealthy. Many people stay together for their children, convenience, or because they are just coping. There is such a thing as a life of misery. Point in case: I knew a couple whose marriage lasted for more than thirty years; however, it was always one sided. The man was a popular man about the town where the couple lived and was known to have several mistresses and outside children. A point that he did not mind letting people know. I remember his stories from childhood. The relationship was filled with abuse emotionally, verbally and physically. Every time his family would take a trip, he would leave the wife at home while the ex-wife would pile up in the car. The relationship was so disrespectful until the abuser would go around bragging about the abuse to family and friends. He told a story of how one day he was beating his wife, and she lay on the ground as if she was dead. He then said that he yelled, "Since you are dead, I'll just go ahead and run over you." She then jumped up and ran across the field. As a child, I had never heard anything more disturbing. Over the years, the abuse continued off and on until one day the wife could no longer take it. In a bizarre rage, while the husband was asleep inside, she took a filled gasoline can and poured gas on her home, set it ablaze and destroyed the home in which the couple lived. The husband managed to escape alive but I never heard him tell another story of abuse. They hospitalized her in a mental facility. She received a visitor while at the facility to check to see how she was doing. She told the visitor that she was not crazy but was just tired and could not take any more. They later released her. What is it to say that you have been in a relationship or married for years when those years are made up of misery? People who choose this path escape the mental facility by finding comfort in a bottle of pills, alcohol, or someone else.

I cannot imagine myself in this type of relationship. We need to remember the time in our youth when we played in the sandboxes or stared out the windows. We never dreamed of a life of misery. We should always remember the little girl and boy that we once were and the promises we made to ourselves "when I grow up . . .." Longevity should not be the only measure of a good relationship or marriage. The key is always to build a marriage that has quality as well as one that will last for years.

# Conclusion

In your quest for "Happily Ever After" and finding, enjoying and keeping real love if you want to have a relationship that is made up of quality, not just quantity. You must love and be your best self. This way, you will be able to share that love with someone else and attract those who want to be with who you are as a person. One can never share what they do not possess. You must simply love yourself. Stop looking for some magical potion or thing. A healthy relationship always starts with you. That is right, "Happily Ever After" begins with you. As stated earlier, you will always be one-half of every relationship you will ever enter into with someone. A healthy you will be part of the foundation of your "House of Love". You should never pretend. The truth will reveal itself in the end. Stop trying to be something or someone you are not. Just Do You! Everyone else is already taken. Your uniqueness makes you special. There is someone for everyone. Once upon a time, people had me thinking there was no one for me in this world. I thought I would never get married or have children. I used to hang around people who made me feel *(from their advice, snickering and jokes)* that I wasn't beautiful enough; my skin wasn't light enough; my parents were not wealthy enough; my butt and tits were not big enough, and my values were not lax enough. Some men felt I wasn't submissive enough; however, this was because I refused to be in a relationship with them while they had sex with other people in the streets and then let them have sex with me. The killing thing about it is that some women gave me the same advice about "letting a man be a man". The truth is there is nothing but potential death, drama and heartache in that. I refused to live as a second class citizen because I was a woman. I had seen the horrors these choices bring, and I wanted no parts of it. The people were liars, and when I cut them out of my life the haze was gone, and I could finally see.

You must be approachable. You cannot receive your blessings in life if no one can approach you. An opportunity has to have a reason to knock on your door. People will perceive you to be approachable if you are open, friendly, and happy.

You need to get to know the other person and their situation to determine if they are the right one for you. They just might be the right one for someone else. It will also be part of your foundation in your "House of Love". Real love is never where it does not exist. Remember to pay attention to the signs. The "Know" is always in the "Show". If they truly love you and want a relationship with you, you will not have to make or try to change them. You will know it and will not have to wonder or guess. Check things out and don't settle. Get out of relationships that are one-sided. Why would you waste your time and allow someone to be worth your valuable time when you are obviously not worth their time by their actions. Also, stop giving it up to every man or woman you meet. Seek to have vertical relationships not horizontal. There are consequences, and the risks are just too high.

As mentioned earlier, you cannot build a healthy relationship without the right mate. It will be like trying to make potato soup without the potatoes. You can consult all the relationship experts in the world and read all the books on the shelves regarding relationships and what men and women think or want, but if you do not choose the right mate, it will be a waste of time. Choosing the right partner is one of the main ingredients in a healthy relationship. As I stated earlier, relationships are not hard; however, being in a relationship with the wrong person is hard. Always choose the right partner so that they will be able to return the love that you deserve. In addition to the right mate, you should be trying to build a "dream" team of greatness, not one filled with nothing but drama and "steam". A Greatness Dream Team is people that add some value to you that: Love You, Motivate You, Encourage You, Inspire You, Enhance You, Make You Happy, and some who are Smarter Than You. It is essential to your growth.

Foundation and structure alone will not upkeep a house or a home. To maintain, you will need something to hold it together. You must have the Acronym TRUST (*T*alk, *R*espect, *U*nderstanding, *S*haring, and *T*olerance), put in the work and pay attention to the signs because a relationship will not function correctly without them. The real secret is that there is no secret. It will be the maintenance that will provide the upkeep for your "House of Love". Do not let anyone tell you different. It is good common sense and hard work. It is worth it! I know what statistic reveal about the trend of marriages and relationships today; however, I like the Bible and the great philosopher, Socrates, am a firm believer that healthy relationships and marriage can and do exist. In these relationships and divorces, you can bet that risk factors were many and one or more of the essential, key ingredients, mainly, choosing the right mate was missing from the recipe mix. Socrates coined a quote that has become famous that says, *"My advice to you is get married: if you find a good wife* (choosing the right mate) *you'll be happy; if not, you'll become a philosopher"*. Wisdom from the Wise, who apparently chose wrong. The essential, vital elements mentioned in this guide along with our faith have served my husband and me well over the years. "The proof is in the pudding," my grandmother would say. As I mentioned earlier, my husband and I have enjoyed many years of marriage during which time we did not separate from each other. My husband says that he prayed for someone that would bring him love, peace, and happiness that he could spend the rest of his life enjoying. I prayed that a good man would come my way, and I am very thankful that God granted me the wisdom to be myself and recognize him when he did come my way. There is something to say about a family that prays together. They usually stay together. It is a good thing to wake each day and to be able to say, I "still" enjoy and love you after all the years. In life's journey of love, quality beats quantity every time. That is not to say we have not had trials. We had to overcome obstacles in life like all couples. Some of them have had a profound impact on our lives, but it was the essential, key elements in this book that allowed us to weather life's bitter storms. We both recognize it would have been easier had we did a few things differently.

Life and relationships are never always a bed of roses; however, living "happily ever after" is reachable by building a structure and foundation and maintaining your "House of Love" that will allow you and your mate's relationship to stay healthy and weather the storms of life. It will certainly make your journey in life easier. Be a visionary. Make an investment in yourself, be approachable, choose the right person and situation for you and protect your investments on your path to turn your dream of finding, enjoying and keeping real love into a reality. Until next time smile, surround yourself with greatness, spread love, and stay blessed and encouraged. Stay up-to-date by visiting www.jblovebooks.com or "jblovebooks" on Facebook. Follow me on Twitter: MuchLoveFromJLove @ForeverLove4All.

# Questions You Must Know the Answers to Before You Jump:

❖ Are either of you already in a serious relationship or marriage? _____ If the answer is "yes", there is no need to finish this list at this point as it relates to the person in question.

❖ Where will we live? _____ If you both already have a property, on which property will you live or will you sell and start a new?

_____

❖ If you are religious, what religion will you follow and church will you attend? _____

_____

❖ Where will you spend holidays? In some relationships, one mate forces the other to give up family celebration yearly as opposed to alternating:

    Thanksgiving _____
    Christmas _____
    Fourth of July _____
    Other: _____ _____

❖ Will you have children, when, how many and how will they be raised, educated and disciplined?

_____

❖ In some cases, how many children do you already have? _____

❖ How will you respond to close relatives who will be your in-laws? _____

_____

❖ Will there be a prenuptial agreement? _____

❖ How much debt will each of you bring into the relationship, what are your plans to reduce it, and how do you feel about making future purchases on credit? _____

❖ How will you as a couple make financial decisions? Who will manage the household budget, make sure all the bills are paid, and write the checks? _____

_____

❖ Do you want to work outside the home after getting married? _____

❖ Do either of you see sex as only a duty or how do each of you feel about intimacy? _____

_____

❖ What do you expect from each other? _____

_____

❖ List any major illnesses_____

_____

❖ Did you leave their last mate because they became ill or lost their job? _____

## My Real Love Traits List

*(Traits are distinguishing quality or characteristics belonging to a person. You can't change a person. You can only change those things you can that want to see in yourself. If they do not have what is most important on your list, they are not the right person for you. Keep it moving.)*

o   <u>Loving</u>

o   <u>Self-Sufficient</u>

o   <u>Confident</u>

o   <u>Secure</u>

o   _____

o   _____

o   _____

o   _____

o   _____

o   _____

o   _____

o   _____

o   _____

o   _____

# REFERENCE

Dysfunctional family - Wikipedia, the free encyclopedia (n.d.). Retrieved October 1, 2010 from https://en.wikipedia.org/wiki/Dysfunctional_family